Radical Housing Solutions

A Plan to *Fix* America's Housing Crisis

Tony Bonitati

Speak It To Book

www.speakittobook.com

Radical Housing Solutions / Tony Bonitati
ISBN-13: 978-1-945793-66-0

Praise for Tony Bonitati and
Radical Housing Solutions

"Tony has a true insider's perspective into the housing crisis we are facing here in the U.S. He has some unique ideas and concepts that when applied, will positively impact the next generation of homeowners. He has packed the book full of solid strategies, backed by years of experience, wisdom, and success. Whether you are looking to purchase your first home, or are an experienced investor, this book is a well thought-out guide to help you navigate the stormy waters of residential property."

John Hawkins
Leadership Speaker
Author of *Expect Greatness: Living a Life of Excellence*

CONTENTS

rad·i·cal

noun

"(especially of change or action) relating to or affecting the fundamental nature of something; far-reaching or thorough"

(e.g., *a radical overhaul of the current way of doing things*)

characterized by departure from convention; innovative[1]

hous·ing

noun

shelter or lodging

dwellings for people

a protective covering[2]

so·lu·tions

noun (pl.)

means of answering or resolving a problem

ways out of a difficult situation

4 · TONY BONITATI

The New Movement for Homeownership

Thank you for picking up a copy of this book. My ultimate goal in writing *Radical Housing Solutions* is to increase the number of homeowners in America, specifically among our younger generations. It is also my sincere hope that you learn something that can help you bring about change in your community.

Even if your goal is to have more flexibility in life, and not to own a home, this book is still for you. Everyone should have the freedom and opportunity to live out their American dream, and owning a home is the backbone of making that dream a reality. For some, it's a way to build wealth. For others, stability.

This book provides stepping stones that will kick-start

the housing market and help millions of Americans who struggle each day to pay their rent.

My hope is that after reading this book, you will have the skills to pay down your student loans, save for a down payment, and even help those who are vulnerable in your community. In many ways, our homeless crisis in America is one of the most pressing issues of our time.

More housing for all income levels will improve our ability to put a roof over every person's head, whether that person can afford it or not. So, if you have a passion for community leadership, this book will teach you how to bring about change through understanding the issue better.

Please join me in this radical challenge, and together we will work to transform the landscape of homeownership in America.

CHAPTER ONE

The American Dream

A man is not a whole and complete man unless he owns a house and the ground it stands on.[3]

—Walt Whitman

The writers of the Declaration of Independence may not have mentioned it alongside "Life, Liberty, and the Pursuit of Happiness," but owning a home has long been a fundamental part of the American Dream. For most of our history, in fact, it *embodied* that dream.

What is that dream, the promise of America? That anyone from anywhere can build a life and prosper through sheer hard work and will. And how do know you when you've succeeded? When you have your own house with a white picket fence.

The American Revolution largely began as a dispute over just who owned the land—and by extension, the houses on it. Following the Civil War, when land prices skyrocketed due to a lack of space in overcrowded Eastern cities, millions of people risked injury, disease, and death to head West. Determined to start new lives for themselves, these settlers tamed new lands to build new houses, claiming and cultivating an entire continent in the process. The United States evolved out of a desire for every citizen to have a place of his or her own.

But our homes are more than just status symbols. They are deeply linked to feelings of family and security. We start our marriages, raise our children, celebrate birthdays, holidays, and milestones there. When we finally retire, we spend our time "puttering around the house," making small repairs, gardening, and enjoying the place that a lifetime of hard work built—or bought. In these divisive times, when it seems like we can't agree on *anything*, owning a home is maybe the one shared goal we have left. And for a large number of Americans, that goal is going to be impossible to attain.

I'm not talking about the growing number of the poor in the United States. Much has been written—and not nearly enough done—about the effects of insufficient mental health care, wage stagnation, gentrification, and the myriad other problems leading to homelessness. Like all Americans, the poor also deserve a place to call their own without the daily stress or worry about whether they can afford and maintain it.

But this book is about an entire generation of young people who are being victimized by a perfect storm of financial factors. For the much-maligned generation known as millennials, there will be no house with a white picket fence unless we take action now.

Of course, it sometimes *seems* like we have too many houses. Like in 2006, when the real estate bubble began to burst; or in rural America where homes are simple boarded up and abandoned; or when thousands of newly-built, relatively-expensive apartments cropped up in our cities.

When I say not enough houses, let me clarify. I'm talking about a lack of available homes at every income level. I believe we have strayed from the basics of housing in America, putting extravagance over need, and many have suffered, or will suffer, the consequences if we don't act.

A Long View from Long Experience

This may sound alarmist, but let me assure you that I know a thing or two about this subject. I've worked in the real estate field for thirty-five plus years, in various capacities. In fact, I bought my first piece of land—literally, one square inch of land—from an advertisement at the back of a comic book when I was about 10 years old. For five dollars, I became the proud owner of a square inch of land somewhere out West—I even got a deed to prove it.

This was in the 1970s. My mother worked as a real estate agent at the time. A few years after she got started in the business, she and my father purchased a duplex as a rental property. When a tenant moved out, I helped them with the painting and cleaning so a new tenant could move in. The experience taught me the first and arguably the most important lesson of the business: you can't own property unless you're willing to get your hands dirty.

My unofficial internship in property management led me to a finance degree—which included several classes in real estate—at Arizona State University. While still in school, at age 22, I came across a listing for a 600-square-foot condo in a new building and, with my parents as co-signers, purchased it for $60,000. I lived there with rent-paying roommates for a year and a half—long enough to graduate and get married—before purchasing my second home, a foreclosure that needed work, at auction for $73,000. The price was a good bit below the average in that neighborhood at the time.

Purchasing a home at auction is both exciting and dangerous. There could be big expenses hiding inside the walls or under the ground. Luckily, we had a friend in construction who visited the property with us before we bid.

The next home was another step forward for me, well, us—a spacious four-bedroom, two-bath fixer-upper that, as my wife recalls, "had a funky smell." But the purchase price was roughly two times our annual income at the time—unthinkable in today's market, where the purchase price of a home can be four or five times your annual income. Those first forays into property ownership began a varied, sometimes rambling career in real estate.

Most recently, I've spent the majority of the last decade as a commercial real estate broker focused on selling multifamily properties for NAI Earle Furman, a leading brokerage firm. Here, I've also enjoyed training young college graduates in all aspects of commercial real estate, including sales, financial analysis, and macroeconomic real estate trends. I've been a licensed broker in North and South Carolina since 2010. Before that, I bought and sold individual properties and handled leases for other corporations like Maytag.

Our family still owns several single-family home rentals today. In total, I have sold, helped developers build, and remodeled over half a billion dollars in real estate, including thousands of apartment units, multi-family developments, single-family homes, and other properties.

I've experienced a lifetime of highs and lows—none lower than the 2008 housing crisis that still impacts the market today. I've made mistakes, and a few smart calls, too. At various times throughout my career, I've been both the problem and the solution in American housing and, as such, I am uniquely qualified to recognize just how dire the situation might become if we don't act very, very soon.

I've also had a pretty good sense of market trends, which has helped me capitalize on being ahead of the curve, so to speak, in real estate. Therefore, I've also included long-term predictions regarding the future of American housing in the last chapter of this book. Some future trends may begin while I'm still alive to see them, but others will likely take another generation to materialize.

The Overcomplicated Necessities of Life

In the introduction to this chapter, we invoked the phrase "Life, Liberty, and the Pursuit of Happiness." Now let's compare that idea to the three basic needs: food, clothing, and shelter. Modern American culture has blown each of these needs out of proportion. One does not have to look hard at our country's love affair with food to see that it has become problematic. We've super-sized food, glamorized it, and processed the heck out of it. Instead of being our daily bread, food has become a customized smorgasbord of overindulgence.

Clothing? Well, I decided to bag up some of the old clothes I had in my closet. I don't know about you, but even after tossing two or three black trash bags full of clothing, I still have literally hundreds of items to wear. Sadly, I also counted over forty pairs of shoes and sneakers. I'm the first to admit I hate throwing old shoes away—you just never know when you might need them.

Let's turn our attention now to the basic necessity of shelter. This perspective may ruffle a few feathers, but we have taken the customization of shelter too far. I'm a big fan of developers and of home improvement retailers. In fact, my uncle had a family business of building custom homes.

There is a place for customized homes in society, and everyone should have the freedom to build any size home he or she wants. However, we have sacrificed basic dwellings in favor of an overreaching customized system of housing, which includes ground up construction and existing home remodeling.

I liken this twenty-year trend to how we view our smartphones. Recall how we only had hardwire home phones for most of the twentieth century. Our biggest decision was whether to get a wall mount phone or a tabletop phone. Then we got to pick from different colors, wow!

In the same vein, housing was of similar construction—basic two- or three-bedroom designs with one or two bathrooms—with variations by region, such as Cape

Cod style in New England and single-story homes with a patio in Florida.

Then, as with cell phones and now smartphones, our options in housing styles and sizes became unlimited. The iPhone is an amazing device, but we will most likely toss our current phone in a few years to get the latest and greatest iPhone for a few hundred bucks more. The same is not true for your customized house. You build it, it's going to last forty or more years, even after you move out.

Just as food and clothing have become so much more than basic necessities, so has the modern home—be it single family or a new apartment building. Most of our housing construction of the last twenty years has generally become too large, too expensive, or both. What we need in housing now are basic starter home neighborhoods all across the country. As I will explain in this book, it is much harder to make money selling smaller homes, so builders simply don't.

It was time for me to write this book because the generation known as the millennials is facing a grim financial future. Not only are many millennials underemployed, but they are crushed by student loans that are preventing them from making the dream of homeownership a reality, "with a new study saying 89 percent plan to purchase a home in the future—but simply can't because of student debt."[4]

Not everyone will be a homeowner in the future, but even renters are struggling more now, compared to the last few decades. Most importantly, I firmly believe that the difference in an individual's future net worth, along with his or her ability to possibly retire after thirty or forty years of work, is homeownership.

The Survey of Consumer Finances states that, in the year 2016, homeowners had an average net worth of $231,400 and renters had an average net worth of $5,200 (see Figure 1). The difference between the two is forty-five-fold, with an ever-increasing gap—between 2013 and 2016, homeowners had a 15 percent increase, while renters had a 5 percent decrease in average net worth. The fact that homeownership drives the wealth of the middle class in America is well known. Paying off a mortgage monthly essentially means that anything individuals pay beyond the interest accumulates "savings."

Homeownership is increasingly difficult to achieve, however, because homes are becoming more expensive while the average income of middle-class Americans is remaining the same. The average income for a family in 1965 was $6,882, while an average new home cost only about three times this much, about $20,000, as documented by the Census Bureau.[5]

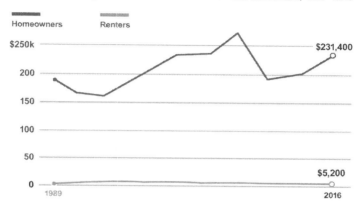

Home ownership is the engine of American wealth

Median inflation-adjustment net worth of home owners and renters, 1989 - 2016

Figure 1. This fact is widely confirmed: homeowners are much better off financially than renters are![6]

We face a critical shortage of homes for first-time buyers, and this will soon impact every aspect of American life. But this impending crisis also affords an opportunity for meaningful change *if* we take decisive and radical action right now. This book outlines eleven radical solutions that will help us subvert this crisis. At the end of each chapter, application-focused workbook sections will help you brainstorm about your role in implementing these solutions. I should also say that despite, or perhaps because of, my experience in this industry, I believe that we *will* solve this problem.

Despite our differences, Americans have always shown the ability to come together with great fortitude and creativity when the moment requires it. I hope the ideas presented in this book can open the door for dialogue and helpful change.

Chapter One Questions

Question: What does homeownership mean to you personally? How has it impacted your life—past, present, and plans for the future?

_____

_____

_____

_____

_____

_____

_____

_____

_____

_____

Question: Why do you think homeownership is such an integral part of the American Dream?

_____

_____

_____

_____

_____

_____

_____

_____

_____

_____

_____

Question: In what ways have we taken the customization of shelter too far?

_____

_____

_____

_____

_____

_____

_____

_____

CHAPTER TWO

From Crash to Crisis

Not so long ago, America was struggling to crawl out of an economic collapse so devastating, it cracked the very foundation of its financial system. A precipitous stock market crash led to a rash of bank closings, home evictions, and a soaring unemployment rate, to say nothing of a pervasive, shared feeling that America was teetering on the brink of total collapse.

That description likely calls back memories—or more accurately, nightmares—of the financial crisis of 2008–2009, but I'm actually referring to the Great Depression. In late October 1929, the Dow Jones dropped twenty-five percent over four days, setting off a chain of events that would cripple the world economy.[7] [8] It would take nearly a decade and another World War for America to recover. But recover we would, leading to arguably the most successful period for middle-class families in the country's history in the 1950s.

There are compelling parallels to be drawn between the

post-Depression era and our current economic reality. But to expect a similar return to the widespread prosperity of 1950s America is dangerous and misguided. Let's take a closer look at the reasons why.

Imagine for a moment that you are a young male returning home from World War II. Despite your brutal experiences overseas, you return to a country nearly delirious with joy and relief. Peace, seemingly definitive this time, reigns even as the "benefits" of that devastating war—e.g., a manufacturing boom—have finally freed the economy from its post-Depression malaise. Assuming you're white, you'll have no trouble finding a job that pays enough to start and support a family. You'll also reap the benefits of President Roosevelt's G.I. Bill, which will fund a college education, should you choose to attend, and offer low-interest home loans. Indeed, it seems as though events have conspired to afford you a comfortable, materially satisfying adult life, perhaps as a sort of karmic payback for what you have endured.

And so, you take advantage, joining the ranks of a "middle-class" of Americans that can survive, even thrive, on one income. You marry, buy a car and a starter home and then have children—lots of children. About 77 million children were born between 1946 and 1964, the aptly-named baby boomer generation.[9] Time passes, and you buy a nicer car and a bigger home. These are things you can afford, after all; from 1950 to 1960, the median home value rose from $7,300 to $11,000, while the median household income, grew in a manner that allowed it to remain at roughly half the amount of the median home value.[10]

In a very real sense, the modern idea of the American Dream stems from this period. For many Americans, prejudices and discrimination have always put this dream beyond reach. And for the rest, it's been dying a slow death ever since. Despite the obvious similarities between the Great Depression and the Great Recession of 2008–2009, even though we exist now in a situation remarkably similar to America circa 1949, we are not poised for the kind of middle-class prosperity and growth that characterized the 1950s.

The reason? A lack of affordable homes, especially for the huge segment of the population that needs them most.

A Dire Warning

Ask any of my friends: I'm a very positive guy. The glass is always half full in my world, hardly ever half empty. But something smells funny. After more than thirty-five years in real estate, I've got a bad feeling in my gut. I've been fortunate and blessed to have been on the cutting edge of the last several real estate trends. Most recently, I was on the front end of the multifamily boom, when large apartment buildings came in high demand. Before that, we sold our home and moved out of Florida right before the housing bubble crashed, and we never looked back.

While my track record is good, it's not perfect. I will confess to selling Apple stock in 2005 at around $11 per share (I think I paid $8 a share). Yes, left a little money on the table with that trade! But, when it comes to real estate,

I picked up something early on. Call it luck, vision, bless-ings, sixth sense, or the culmination of years of building sweat equity from hard work and hard knocks.

Friends, our housing market is simply stuck. Our large economic engine of homeownership has a flashing oil light. And, just like an engine that starts smoking from lack of oil, we don't have long to pull over and fix this.

Millennials have seen a period almost the opposite of the 1970s, with slow or no wage growth, and generally falling prices caused by technology. Think flat-screen TVs, cell phones, and the internet. All of these things have drastically improved our lives, and we have become ac-customed to having next year's version being cheaper and faster.

Millennials, I've got some bad news, and as you've heard: "You ain't seen nothing yet." The big concern is the pendulum always swings too far both ways. The gov-ernment may have overcompensated for the Great Recession by allowing the stimulus and low interest rate era to go on a little too long. We'll see. Unfortunately, we may have all been lulled to sleep about the reality of in-flation, or its really bad cousin, stagflation.

Let me give you my firsthand account of inflation, from when I was growing up. Money was tight around my house when I was teenager. I was a high schooler in 1978 and 1979—yes, disco was all the rage, but I preferred groups like Journey and Styx.

We were a growing family of five, sometimes eating a week's worth of food in a couple of days. Now don't get me wrong, we never were without. But the wages back then could not keep up with the rising prices of necessities. I'll never forget my dad one day, sitting there with the checkbook and muttering, "So, do you want to eat this week, or pay the light bill?" That's what inflation feels like: having to make choices between the basics.

And in our country today, with fifteen percent of our population living below the poverty line, trust me, we are only one bad couple of months away from catastrophe. Think about the phrase "living paycheck to paycheck." Or the headlines saying that fifty-seven percent of our population has less than $1,000 saved.[11] Ouch. So many people are dangerously teetering on the brink of financial disaster.

Is that the dire warning? Stagflation and the marginal running out of money at the end of their paycheck? Nope. That's only the start. If I'm right, and we do not dramatically and radically fix housing now, we are facing a generational shift of economic power worse than the Great Depression.

Even writing those words makes me cringe. Remember, I'm an extremely positive guy. And I believe that, if we take action, we can avert the consequences of this dire warning. But the truth is, we only have a short time to act or we will end up in serious trouble.

While this dire warning may seem a little harsh, it is based on factual data which supports my projection. I hope I'm wrong, but we are facing a dire future if we cannot fix the housing market now. In fact, we have less than a decade. If we are unable to radically change our current housing scenario, we will dramatically alter the future of our country. There are several ways that the status quo will lead to dire consequences.

Just like high school seniors delight in torturing incoming freshmen, every generation delights in disparaging the one that will eventually replace it. But arguably no generation in history has taken more abuse than millennials, and if you're a millennial reading this book, you're probably nodding your head already.

While the term has become a derisive code word for "young people" in general, the word millennials specifically refers to people born between 1981 and 1996, according to the Pew Research Center.[12] Labeled as lazy and entitled, millennials have been blamed for the death of the automobile, beer, cereal, and soap industries, chain restaurants, and department stores—and that's just this week.

So it's ironic that, from a historical perspective, the millennial generation shares quite a bit in common with "the Greatest Generation." Both came of age in the shadow of a tragic historical event (World War II and the 9/11 terrorist attacks) and a world-changing economic downturn (the Great Depression and Great Recession). But unlike young adults starting their lives in the 1950s, millennials, all 84 million of them, lack the benefit of favorable market conditions and social programs like the G.I. Bill to jumpstart their path to homeownership.[13]

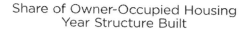

Share of Owner-Occupied Housing
Year Structure Built

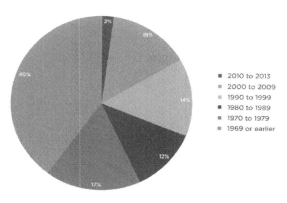

- 2010 to 2013
- 2000 to 2009
- 1990 to 1999
- 1980 to 1989
- 1970 to 1979
- 1969 or earlier

Source: 2013 AHS, U.S. Census Bureau

Figure 2. Homeownership (versus renting) has decreased drastically since the immediate post-WWII decades—with the sharpest decreases after 1969 and after 2009.[14]

You may be a millennial who is wondering why you're 30 years old and haven't yet purchased a home. The wealth and family-building decade of the millennials is upon us, as I will explain in detail—but the truth is, many millennials can barely afford housing at all.

There is no shortage of statistics related to the financial struggles of the average American. It's easy to get buried in a cascade of numbers related to income inequality, the shrinking middle class, lack of retirement and savings, and just about every other indicator of how impossibly expensive life has become for most Americans.

So consider this simple proof instead: The target amount to spend on housing is roughly thirty percent of your monthly income. The latest U.S. census puts the average worker's annual salary between $31,099 and $46,550—a total income of about $2,500 to $3,800 a month before taxes.[15] Sticking to the thirty percent figure, that leaves about $750–$1,100 for housing *before* related expenses like utilities.

Go ahead and try to find a reasonable rent in that price range in most markets, never mind a mortgage payment for your first home. Indeed, only 64.3 percent of Americans own homes, as of July 26, 2018.[16] The number of millennials, specifically, is 37 percent.[17]

Yet millennials make up the largest segment of America's workforce, *despite* struggling with unemployment— or underemployment—because they began looking for their first "adult" jobs in the aftermath of the 2008–2009 recession. After nearly being shut out of the job market, millennials are now being shut out of the most crucial element of the American Dream.

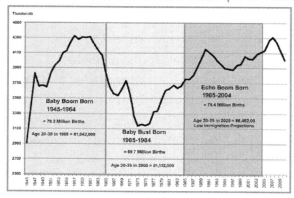

Annual Births in the United States (1945–2010)

Figure 3. The current decrease in fertility rates is similar to the "baby bust" years of the mid-1960s through the early 1980s.[18]

But the problem goes beyond dreams. Housing is a basic human need, like food and clothing. People feel insecure without access to those essential things. And without security, they are less likely to do things like start a family.

This is where the effects of the housing problem start to extend beyond generational boundaries. The fertility rate in the U.S. sank to 60.2 births per 1,000 women in 2017—the lowest level in thirty years, according to the Center for Disease Control.[19] Even more concerning, the birth rate has not risen above the replacement rate—the point at which births surpassed deaths—since 1971.[20]

From a strictly economic standpoint, these trends present a clear and present threat to America's future. Fewer people means fewer workers, which significantly hampers growth. Countries like Japan, Italy, and Macao are currently feeling the effects of this problem.[21] When coupled with a rapidly increasing elderly population, many of whom live at or below the poverty line, programs like Social Security become unsustainable. And the challenges only compound from there.

Putting aside the long-term theoretical implications of our affordable housing problem, millennials face immediate concerns. Being forced to pay rent rather than a mortgage for a home means giving away 30 percent to 50 percent of one's earnings without any return on the investment. Contrary to what we believed pre-2008, the housing market doesn't go up forever, but it is a steady long-term investment. The average home appreciates is 3 percent to 5 percent annually, according to the Federal Housing Finance Agency (FHFA).[22]

We can look at paying a mortgage as a forced savings program—you deposit money into your home, which then builds equity. Homeownership increases a person's net worth and provides a potential nest egg for retirement. To miss out on this investment opportunity is to severely hamper one's personal and potentially long-term family wealth. In other words, once again and through no fault of their own, millennials risk being left out in the cold.

A New Hope

Why *is* homeownership nearly impossible for so many people? The answer is deceptively simple—we don't have enough starter homes for first-time buyers. The Recession of 2008–2009, like the Great Depression before it, created a massive decline in real estate values. This led to a "lost decade" with basically no growth in new homes. Builders wouldn't build; bankers couldn't lend.

Every year, the American economy needs 1.2–1.5 million new homes to keep pace with demand and replace those lost to age, fire, floods, and other types of loss.[23] From 2009–2012, construction ground to a halt, with fewer than 500,000 homes being built in 2009.[24]

Among existing homeowners, the lucky chose to hunker down and hope for the best, while those victimized by the cratering economy—or their own bad mortgages—were evicted. The only markets that saw advances during this painful stretch were apartment buildings—thus creating even more renters with higher renting terms—and high-end luxury houses.

The real estate market has finally emerged from this

period to find the population both under- *and* over-housed. Millennials, as we have discussed, are under-housed, living in expensive rental units that handicap their ability to save for a down payment. And the houses that are available are far too expensive—nothing like the starter homes of decades past.

Meanwhile, aging baby boomers are over-housed in properties way too large for their needs. They believe their homes have tremendous value but fail to understand that value is based on market demand. A 5,000-square-foot, four-bedroom, five-bath McMansion in the suburbs is only worth 1.2 million dollars *if* you have buyers willing and able to pay the asking price.

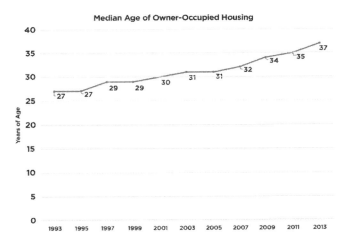

Figure 4. As less new owner-occupied housing is built, the typical age of the existing housing has gradually increased in recent decades.[25]

Construction of new homes has been historically low since 2016, perhaps because builders are afraid of another crash.[26] The fact that there are not enough homes of the proper size available or being constructed has negatively affected household formation. Fewer households are formed,[27] so the actual number of households is significantly below projections.

The housing market has historically operated as a ladder. Young buyers, often couples in their twenties, begin on the lowest rung with an affordable starter home. As these couples age and expand into families, they move up the ladder using their increased worth, both from higher salaries through advancing careers and the equity from their existing property.

The problem we face is that ladder is currently overloaded, keeping everyone on their current rungs and creating a frustrated crowd of renters stranded on the ground waiting to climb. The market is not moving as people have nowhere to go and remain as "stuck" as the housing market.

So, how many additional houses will fix this problem? Ten million. That's the number of affordable, entry-level homes we need in the next ten years[28]—*beyond* the 1.4–1.5 million homes constructed annually on average,[29] considering that two counties in California (Los Angeles and Orange), for instance, have an immediate need for well over half a million affordable homes for low-income households![30]

In other words, we can't build ourselves out of this hole—we need to *find* at least ten million new roofs, a vast network of inexpensive dwellings that can affect values and restart movement up the housing ladder. Doing so will increase supply at all levels of housing, creating a chain reaction of positive effects across socioeconomic classes and age demographics—increased wealth and savings, upward mobility in property ownership, and an easing of out-of-control rental prices.

But to reap those benefits, we'll first need to take a hard, uncomfortable look at our housing expectations and goals. We'll need to tackle our very conceptions of what a home is and can be. Extreme problems require radical solutions.

We can't solve our housing problem by simply ramping up construction. In fact, there is no single *silver bullet* for a problem of this magnitude. Instead, we'll need to rely on creative, perhaps even extreme, proposals to create paradigm shifts in the way we view housing and our own resources. In my research, I have brainstormed eleven radical solutions to begin addressing the housing shortage in America. Solving this crisis requires everyone's participation.

WORKBOOK

Chapter Two Questions

Question: When it comes to finding affordable housing, do you think millennials are at a greater disadvantage than their post-World War II predecessors? Why or why not?

_____

_____

_____

_____

_____

_____

_____

_____

_____

_____

_____

_____

Question: Describe the conditions that have affected either yourself as a millennial, or millennials you know, when it comes to purchasing a first house or climbing the housing ladder. Do you see these experiences as typical for this generation—why or why not?

_____

_____

_____

_____

_____

_____

_____

_____

_____

_____

Question: What are some negative cultural/societal trends that can result from a lack of affordable housing? Have you seen any of these play out in your life or in the lives of those you know?

_____

_____

_____

_____

_____

_____

_____

_____

_____

_____

_____

_____

Action: Without reading further in the book yet, make a list of ideas and strategies you think could help close the gap and meet the need for ten million starter homes.

CHAPTER THREE

Big Problem,
Bigger Opportunities

The most effective way to allow our younger generations an entry to homeownership is to start by improving the affordability of rent. Ultimately, our goal is to "fix" the housing ladder. In order to do so, we will need to increase the number of available homes at every wrung of the ladder.

We believe that private enterprise will benefit once there is more disposable income. Therefore, we start with business-led solutions since the free market is the fastest way to get new ideas implemented.

Radical Solution #1
Employer and Corporation Housing Villages

At the beginning of the twentieth century, and in fact, well into the 1950s and '60s, living where you worked was extremely common. Farmers employed several hands who stayed on site seasonally and sometimes year-round. New England and other regions were dotted with mill towns, so-named because workers often lived in housing villages in close proximity to their mills. These weren't feudal arrangements from the Middle Ages; companies paid their workers and provided housing for free or at a reduced rate.

Growing up in the 1970s in Connecticut, I recall local businesses where employees lived in apartments above the shops, provided by the owners. The lumberyard near my home also had workers who lived on the premises. Employer-provided housing can have positive effects on communities and mobility. EAH (employer-assisted housing), which may also encompass measures like down-payment assistance and loan guarantee programs, can result in a more stable workforce, as well as higher quality of life due to lower commute times and less traffic congestion.[31]

Yet we have steadily moved away from that model. Employers entice prospective workers with other types of benefits—competitive salaries, medical and dental benefits, stock options, etc. In other words, housing is the employee's problem.

Until it isn't. Affordable housing is quickly becoming *the* deciding factor when it comes to companies attracting talented staff. In places like San Francisco and parts of Silicon Valley in California, computer engineers making six figures cannot afford homes within reasonable commuting distance. In desperation, some have reverted to the worker camp model on the sly by living out of cars, moving trucks, or RVs in company parking lots. Other burgeoning tech zones like Boulder, Colorado, and Austin, Texas, are seeing real estate prices spike out of control as well.

Though employer-provided or employer-assisted housing isn't a new concept, it's now a necessary one once more. We're nearing a point where well-qualified employees may turn down higher-paying jobs based on where those jobs are located. In fact, cities like Pittsburgh, Pennsylvania are already trying to capitalize on this sea change with advertising campaigns saying, in essence, "Want a tech job *and* affordable housing? Move to Pittsburgh."[32]

Forward-thinking tech leaders, many of whom pride themselves on "outside the box" thinking and innovation, have a unique opportunity here. Imagine if a certain unnamed Internet company in one of these expensive markets offered free or reduced-rate housing to staff? There are many options for housing with this solution. Employers in different regions can use the type of housing that best fits the needs of their employees, and their community. In some situations where there is an abundance of land, a development of single-family homes or prefabricated homes near a facility could be viable. In other cases, like near Disney World, well-appointed dorms for *all* workers may be a better solution.

My daughter spent a semester of college in the Disney College Internship program in Orlando. During her internship, she worked at one of the theme parks and lived in Disney's employer housing. A sprawling community of thousands of dorm style apartments within a few miles of the theme parks. This housing served many employees including the college interns, international students, and seasonal workers. Disney also conveniently provided transportation for these workers, cutting down on traffic and—more importantly—the expense of even having to own a vehicle. When an employee was off work, the community was within walking distance of grocery stores, restaurants and entertainment. Some older workers might balk at the idea of living like college students, but if you've seen one of these apartment settings, it might surprise you. A shared common space like kitchens and living area with private individual bedroom and bathrooms for multiple people. Even the most skeptical would certainly see the sense of living accommodations that allow them to begin saving toward a down payment on a home, rather than throwing that money away every month in rent.

Employer housing is not a new concept, just one we have not taken advantage of this generation. The goal of employer and corporate housing solutions is to provide a temporary living arrangement for employees so they can save enough in living expenses for a year or two for a down payment on their own home. Employers can then partner with developers to build sustainable long-term communities for these now tenured employees while newly-hired employees move into the employer housing.

Sure, there are challenges to this approach. But considering the shortage of skilled labor, and the ongoing competitiveness of employees, employers could benefit by offering this valuable employee benefit. Another challenge is the long-term sustainability of jobs in a given area. Certainly the rust belt has felt the effect of a combined decline of industry and economic conditions.

The government could incentivize companies to offer such a benefit, which isn't exactly unheard-of. Programs like the Work Opportunity Tax Credit (WOTC) offer thousands of dollars in tax breaks for companies who hire individuals fitting certain criteria, such as veterans and people with disabilities.[33] There are also incentives for reducing commute times, which this concept does. The towns where the employers are located could also add parks, and other services, thereby providing a boost to the local economy. There would be challenges, of course, but the net benefit to both the companies and employees would be substantial.

In terms of housing specifically, the effect would be two-fold. *One*, employer-subsidized housing would relieve demand in over-crowded markets, thus lowering rent prices that have become overwhelming for many workers. We aren't just talking about well-compensated white-collar workers. If a developer for a successful internet company can't afford rent in San Francisco, how will a waitress or retail worker or school teacher survive? Large manufacturing firms would likely decrease turnover and other employee expenses with employer housing.

Two, this type of housing allows young workers to begin saving in earnest toward buying a home and gaining entry to the housing ladder—and all the accrued wealth it might afford.

In short, affordable housing is an incentive that will better a company's chances at recruiting and retaining quality workers. While employers are at risk for turnover when competitors offer slightly higher wages, affordable housing represents a tangible benefit that means more to the employee than a small pay raise.

Commercial Housing Solutions works with companies to offer housing for employees that is significantly below the average market rent. For employees, this strategy generates a larger net income after housing expenses compared to earning a higher salary elsewhere and paid market rent. While utilizing the benefits of Commercial Housing Solutions, employees can start saving money for a down payment to become a homeowner in the near future—and we've got a plan for when that time comes, too!

Please visit our solutions website for more info:

commercialhousingsolutions.com

Radical Solution #2
Retail Conversion and Retrofitting

The dawn of online shopping has led to a retail apocalypse over the last twenty years. Toys R Us, a once-thriving national chain, is only one of several high-profile casualties. As a result, we now have millions of square feet of empty retail space, often in the form of ugly, '70s-era retail parks. But within these community eye-sores lies tremendous potential. They all have much-needed infrastructure—power, water, landscaping, parking. The question becomes, how best to use it?

Current retail workers at places like Walmart, Target and Best Buy typically make less than $15 an hour. Even assuming they work full time—and most of them don't—at $15 an hour, they'll only make $2,600 a month *before* taxes. With that meager wage, they must pay for housing, food, transportation to and from work and other everyday living expenses. Saving for a home under these circumstances is impossible; even rent without a supplement salary from a second job or roommate is unlikely.

Aren't these workers the ideal candidates to take over all this deserted retail space? Retrofitting unused retail space into apartment modules would likely cost less than building corporate-subsidized dormitories from scratch. Nor would the space be used entirely for affordable housing. These retail parks could be converted and updated to mixed-use developments with a modern, walkable look. Store fronts including supermarkets would occupy the first level with housing upstairs and the parking hidden in the middle or below.

If managed properly, these small units could be structured to be affordable for the average hourly wage worker. There's another possibility as well, though one likely to meet with even more resistance. In December of 2017, the U.S. Department of Housing and Urban Development reported that 554,000 people are now homeless across America.[34] This number was attributed to substantial increases in homelessness across many West Coast cities. Several cities and towns have declared a state of emergency to address the issue.

It's no coincidence that homelessness has risen dramatically in some of the most expensive housing markets in the country. Yet, by and large, most maintain a simplistic, downright prejudiced view of the problem. We think of the homeless as victims of their own bad choices or vices and addictions without understanding that, now more than ever, underlying economic factors make homelessness downright inevitable for some people.

The fact is, the difference between a fairly comfortable middle-class lifestyle and abject poverty and homelessness is often just a couple missed paychecks. On average, the American making $45,000 to $69,999 a year has a savings account balance of $2,200 in 2018. For those making less than $25,000, that number drops to $500.[35]

The classic idea of a "rainy day" fund set aside for health emergencies, unexpected car repairs or other types of emergencies has become a pipe dream for most Americans. Now those types of problems can literally be the difference between affording housing or not. To foist the blame on individual spending habits or personal responsibility or any number of other tired arguments misses the point entirely. Rising healthcare prices, skyrocketing housing costs, and low wages have made life prohibitively expensive for a growing segment of Americans. If this seems like an exaggeration, consider the following example.

The average hourly rate for a full-time worker at Walmart, one of the country's largest employers, is $13.38.[36] That works out to a little more than $2,300 a month *before* taxes. In Lincoln, Nebraska—not exactly a prime real estate market—the average rent for a two-bedroom apartment is $911 a month, according to RentCafe, an apartment finding website.[37] If the typical rent in a relatively affordable location consumes almost half of the monthly wages of a full-time employee for a major corporation, then there's an undeniable problem.

If we can begin to accept the true causes of homelessness today, then perhaps the current views toward the problem will change. Currently, many of us *still* visualize the face of homelessness as a drug addict or the stereotypical "wino" sleeping on a park bench with a brown-bag covered bottle. But the reality is something quite different.

That face could just as easily be a young mother (or father) working a full-time job and still unable to afford housing. In fact, if millennials hadn't been able to stay with their parents while they spent those first desperate years following 2008–2009 being under or unemployed, they likely would have become the face of homelessness in America by now.

These misconceptions about the *whos* and *hows* of the problem only increase a widespread "NIMBY" (Not In My Back Yard) attitude that makes meaningful change harder, especially with controversial issues like homelessness. We want societal improvements—fewer poor people, better infrastructure, alternatives to fossil fuels— as long as they are constructed elsewhere.

But with the decline of brick-and-mortar retail in general, and the demise of many shopping malls in particular,[38] we could likely house every homeless person in America in repurposed, otherwise vacant retail spaces and still have millions of square feet left over.[39] Retail establishments long past their prime, like Landmark Mall in Northern Virginia, are already being given a new lease on life as part of their empty space shelters people, including young families, facing difficult circumstances and limited options.[40]

Unfortunately, proposals of this sort are typically shot

down by the same communities complaining about the ugly empty shopping malls and strips within their towns and cities.

I propose a three-part plan that would engage the entire community:

Step 1: Organize teams of local officials and developers.

Step 2: Identify unused retail properties in local communities.

Step 3: Create a long-term plan.

Commercial brokers would play an essential role in the process in educating and converting local community members. The property owners would likely be an easier sell since vacant buildings do not generate income. Whether the proposed residents be low-income residents or members of the homeless community, the retail property solution can be a big piece of the puzzle in fixing the affordable housing shortage.

Radical Solution #3
Reshape Our Urban Cores

We live in a beautiful mid-size city that had a growing population for over a decade. Our city center has wonderful park system extending along our river banks. Many cities have turned their focus back to a centralized park atmosphere, copying perhaps the most iconic park of all,

Central Park in New York. We absolutely need to grow and preserve green space in our cities.

What we need to reconsider is how much space we waste for automobiles. According to Eran Ben-Joseph, who is a professor of urban planning at M.I.T., "in some U.S. cities, parking lots cover more than a third of the land area, becoming the single most salient feature of our built landscape."[41] A 2018 study by the Research Institute for Housing America found that Seattle has approximately two public parking spaces per household, Philadelphia has four spaces per household, and Des Moines, Iowa, has *nineteen* spaces per household![42]

Without changing any of the streets for moving vehicles, we could free up thousands of acres in our urban core by removing parking space. Stay with me, I'm as American as the next guy, and I love driving my convertible. But when it comes down to parking an SUV for eight hours Monday through Friday versus housing an individual, I hope we can at least agree a roof over someone's head is more important.

I'm not suggesting we change our entire way of life. People should be able to drive wherever and whenever they choose. However, considering how quickly technology in vehicles is changing, we would be crazy to think that our mode of transportation now will be the same in a decade—it won't be. So, here is my radical solution for increasing density in our urban cores: begin with the conversation and elimination of excess parking spaces and structures.

"Wait," you say, "we don't even have enough parking in downtowns today as it is! Now you want less?" Yup.

I'm suggesting we simply begin to move parking a few miles out of the city center. Plus, the coming automotive technological changes will enable us to change our cities much quicker than we think. Ride sharing, autonomous vehicles, and other new options for getting around town will decrease our reliance on individual cars.[43]

When you consider how much land we dedicate to parking in our urban cores, it almost seems obvious. We have so many parking spaces in America it's hard to even count them all. According to some experts, we have as many as two billion parking spaces![44] For every two parking spaces we move off-site, we can create space for housing.

Let's start with a simple example. We displace the top two floors of any city garage (who likes to drive all the way to the top anyway?). We lose maybe one hundred parking spaces, but free up room for up to eighty dwelling units per parking garage. This kind of shift can have an immediate effect on affordability.

Scratching the Surface

None of these three ideas is without its challenges, and indeed, none will single-handedly resolve our housing shortage. But they represent a multi-pronged starting point, one of purposely ambitious scope. Each idea will require unprecedented levels of cooperation and compromise from government officials, businessowners, developers, and many others. It would be a mistake, however, to leave a problem this significant solely in the hands of other people. After all, the struggle for affordable housing now affects all but the wealthiest Americans. So it should fall to all of us to solve it.

WORKBOOK

Chapter Three Questions

Question: Which of the author's proposed solutions in this chapter would be most impactful in your community? How could it work, in practical terms, and what might be the greatest hindrance to this change?

_____

_____

_____

_____

_____

_____

_____

_____

_____

_____

Question: What do you foresee as objections or possible downsides to corporate/employer housing? How can these objections best be overcome, and how can potential downsides be prevented?

_____

_____

_____

_____

_____

_____

_____

_____

_____

_____

_____

Action: Identify a large, vacant structure in your community that could be repurposed into affordable housing. Research examples of how this has been done effectively in other areas.

_____

_____

_____

_____

_____

_____

_____

_____

_____

_____

_____

_____

Action: Talk to local charity organizations (such as Salvation Army, United Way, and Habitat for Humanity), as well as local school administrators, about the causes of homelessness in your community. Ask them to share examples of families who have become homeless due to extenuating circumstances. Evaluate your attitudes toward the homeless and find a few concrete ways to best help those in need.

CHAPTER FOUR

A Multi-Generation Problem

The 1950s did more than usher in a period of widespread—primarily white—middle-class prosperity. It transformed the entire concept of prosperity in a way that future decades would build upon.

Growing up in the 1970s, I clearly remember arriving home in the family's Ford Maverick after grocery shopping. My job was always to get out of the car and "open the garage," which in those days meant literally pulling up the garage door with my hands. Then came remote control garage door openers, which quickly took over. The manual doors were soon obsolete.

It's a trivial example of a significant trend in housing—features and services that start out as luxuries quickly become standard. Sprinkler and irrigation systems, monthly pest control and home security services—we continue to add to the cost of homeownership. As this has happened, size has also increased dramatically.

Starter homes used to be under 1,000 square feet in the

1950s. By 2016, the average size had risen to around 2,500 square feet.[45] A young family of four today squabbles over sharing two bathrooms, when just forty years ago, families twice that size got by with just one.

The following ideas may seem deflationary in nature, but in large part, that's due to the absurd *inflation* of our expectations over the last several decades. In other words, it's time to re-think our needs *and* our expectations of what a home is. The housing shortage is too widespread and our window to act is too short to sit idly by and wait for a cushy and comfortable idea to fix the problem.

Baby boomers are reluctant to downsize, which is causing a huge problem in the housing market. While there are certainly other reasons why baby boomers do not sell their homes, like the preference to stay in the place they have grown accustomed to, the desire to retain home equity, as well as the absence of viable housing alternatives, it is possible that some baby boomers remain in their present housing situation due to mortgage debt.

Boston College's Center for Retirement Research analyzed census data to reveal that, in 2015, the likelihood of individuals over 60 having mortgage debt was more than three times higher than it had been in 1980. Those who have failed to pay off their mortgages by the time they retire are likely to have no pensions and low incomes. There are many challenges associated with staying in homes that are simply not equipped to meet the future needs of their aging occupants, especially regarding healthcare.[46]

For housing, a reset is coming. We have far too many older structures, far too few skilled workers, and far too many barriers to build locally. Radical solutions such as mass-producing dwellings and temporarily placing those units in strategic locations will help alleviate the affordability crunch facing many cities today. Continuing on the path of the last decade will not cut it.

Radical Solution #4
Baby Boomers, It's Time to Sell

Baby boomers, you have been told your whole lives that owning a home is important, and that is true. However, is the equity in your home substantial enough to allow you to live somewhere else for years to come and never mow the lawn again?

Liquidity, namely the possession of money or assets that can be turned into money quickly, should be your new goal. Sell your big house—you can take your memories with you—and be free to take some time to consider your many options. Even if you rent a new apartment for the next few years, the improved lifestyle in a housing setting that suits your current needs, desires, and abilities will make you wonder why you waited. Why should you move before you know where you will be next? Because, the very act of staying somewhere when it's time to move on keeps you from thinking freely.

Consider reading *Who Moved My Cheese* by Spencer Johnson. It worked for me and my family when we were all feeling it was time to move again, but we were reluctant to leave our comfortable situation. Let me tell you, that move saved us from scary things we could not see on the horizon, things that affected some dear friends and family members at the time. Unemployment hit ten percent, and the foreclosure rates hit historical highs Around us, we saw financial stress causing family strife and even divorce. We witnessed the loss of jobs, cars, and homes.[47]

For us, however, this time turned out to be one of the best experiences—all because we jumped at the height and thus had extra money from selling and moving that helped us weather that time. In fact, I too was "laid off" from my job at the end of 2009. If we had not sold, we would have struggled like many who did lose their job but could not sell, because their house was worth less than they paid for it.

Millennials, plan to be an owner. Renting is good for the short term, but you should sacrifice a nicer place today to save for a down payment. Are you already doing that? Ask yourselves, where in the country can you go right now and live more affordably? If your family situation allows it and you are willing to make a move, can you start a path of prosperity by moving every two to four years? I believe you can. There are many options available to you, our largest generation ever. You are the future leaders— be flexible, mobile, and ready to strike.

However, please don't overpay just to own a house. Not all purchases are good ones. I've learned in over five decades of living, including raising a family and buying homes, that a couple of mistakes can cost you the difference between financial independence and financial ruin. Your time to buy a home will come. But first, we must plan to add affordable homes, so you can save for the coming wave of starter homes over the next few years.

The same members of the baby boomer generation who benefited from a favorable confluence of factors when they were young must now be enlisted to ease the burden on millennials today.

To be blunt, boomers need to sell their homes.

I can almost hear the sound of this book being snapped closed—or the Kindle being switched off. For most boomers, the idea of giving up their homes to solve someone else's problem seems downright offensive. Aside from the emotional attachment they have for the site of so many wonderful memories, they also view their house as a valuable financial asset—maybe the most valuable one they have. All those hard-earned mortgage payments, coupled with steady appreciation, are one big equity paycheck that they can cash or pass on to their children. In fact, the very subject of this book—the dearth of housing—seems to reinforce the tremendous value of one's home.

Except the truth isn't quite that simple. What seems like an unfair sacrifice on behalf of a younger generation is actually an act of self-preservation. Remember, we have a massive shortage of new homes in large part because the housing ladder is stuck. The natural progression of a young couple buying a starter home, living there for an average of seven years and then moving out—and up— has ground to a halt. And so those people currently standing at the top rung of the ladder in their lovely, sprawling, suburban houses are about to face a harsh reality.

Despite the impressively high appraisal of a home's value, the owner risks losing a huge portion of their investment over the next several years, because there are simply not enough buyers farther down the ladder who can afford to buy such a property.

The average age of a home-buyer now is 44, not 30, as it was in the 1980s. That's nearly fifteen years of lost equity that could be used toward purchasing a house like yours.[48] This means that in three years' time, a home may be worth less than the original purchase price paid years ago.

Now here's the good news—there's still time. If a home is paid off, the owners should take advantage of the tax law which allows them to shelter their entire capital gain.[49] In other words, sell that $500,000 (or more) home. Build a smaller home for less than your sales amount, say forty percent to fifty percent of the size/cost, and live off the remaining money. This would allow those stuck in the middle of the ladder to move up. It would introduce new non-luxury homes to the market and, hopefully, allow those on the lower rungs of the ladder— or those not on the ladder at all—a chance to make a shift of their own.

Of course, not all baby boomers think of their homes as bank vaults in disguise. Some people enjoy the security in their paid-off property, even if it is too large for their current needs. They take comfort in having a home to grow old in, a place they can afford without the hard work of making those onerous mortgage payments. But this model only works if people can afford the home and its upkeep as they age.

As many reach the fixed-income stage of their later years, this isn't an option. Small tasks like lawncare, larger expenses like roof or boiler repairs, and property taxes can consume a significant part of a baby boomer's reduced income. Money needed to survive ends up being used to pay for maintaining a home.

Currently, sixty million people collect monthly Social Security checks. This number will continue to balloon, with no clear plan to fund it in sight. The monthly payment for an individual receiving Social Security is about $1,300—that's not very much.[50] For many homes, that amount wouldn't cover the property tax, let alone basic upkeep and routine maintenance.

Too often, we overlook the costs of having a home, even when the mortgage is paid off. Seniors are the fastest growing segment of poor people in America, yet many of them are literally sitting on a potential windfall that could solve their financial woes.

Of course, selling your home creates another problem. We've touched on the housing shortage—and if baby boomers *en masse* decide to sell their homes, even to great profit, where exactly will they live?

Radical Solution #5
ADUs, Tiny Homes, Granny Suites, and Mobile Living

A small but vocal *minimalist* trend has been gaining traction in some demographics across the country. The movement seeks to strip away the suffocating material excesses of modern society. If money can't buy you happiness, the idea goes, then neither can the stuff you buy with it. An offshoot of this philosophy is the "tiny house" movement, wherein people construct and live in homes no bigger than 400 square feet.[51] Don't want to be buried in material possessions? Live in a home where those possessions literally can't even fit.

The idea of a tiny house—or even a modest one—may induce skeptical eye-rolls, but at its heart, the trend is no more extreme than the sprawl it opposes. Middle-class families in suburban homes likely have individual bedrooms bigger than 400 square feet and for no purpose other than a decades-long trend of "keeping up with the Joneses." Bringing our super-sized home expectations back to reality doesn't hurt anyone, *and* it will fuel creative solutions to our housing shortage.

Here's just one example: California, which bears some of the least affordable housing markets in the country, has been progressive in rezoning for Accessory Dwelling Units (ADUs). If adopted by the rest of the country, these small units could significantly ease the housing shortage among two crucial segments of the population—aging baby boomers and young workers. If laws allow, a small apartment could easily be partitioned out of today's sprawling suburban home, similar to the in-law apartments or "granny suites" of decades past.

In many cases, creating this apartment could be as simple as converting space above the omnipresent two-car garage or building a small home elsewhere on a single-family property.

This could be an option for the elderly, whether they're looking to enjoy a comfortable retirement after selling their property, still drowning under the expenses of a home they can no longer afford, or struggling to pay rent on a fixed income. Millennials, unable to afford housing, could also benefit from an apartment above the garage or similar tiny home situation.

Matching prospective tenants to landlords could even be need-based and utilize technology, the way Airbnb revolutionized vacation rentals. Imagine a "Granny Suite Finder" app, where millennials are matched to aging baby boomers in need of a dog walker, cook, or landscaper. Think of the ancillary benefits of adding "new blood" to the staid, homogeneous suburb experience.

These additional roofs do more than help on an individual or even community level. They create vacancies in lower-end apartments, rental homes, and even workforce housing, thus lowering prices. Lower rents, as we have discussed, decrease homelessness and lower the cost burden on young adults looking to save for their first homes. The sooner they can step onto the housing ladder, the better their chances to build sustained wealth. The positive effects go on and on.

ADUs

The legal term ADU refers to a secondary living space that contains its own entrance, kitchen, and living area and can be rented separately, but is located on the lot of a primary house, either attached to the house or garage, or built as its own unit. The ADU usually shares the energy and water connections of the larger house. In recent years, the ADU has come up as a solution to contain the urban sprawl while still providing adequate housing for a growing, economically diverse population.

While previous zoning rules prohibited or hindered the creation of ADUs, new zoning rules allow for ADUs while limiting their size and style options. The rules usually also state that the owner of the primary house has to live on the plot. In cities like Portland, Oregon, the building of ADUs is encouraged by means of lowered costs of necessary building permits.[52]

Our radical solution is for all states and local governing bodies to immediately relax zoning laws for ADUs. In almost every urban area in the country, we can house fifty percent more people by allowing the rapid expansion of ADUs. California, leading the way, passed its law January 1, 2018. California relaxed its ADU codes in 2017, leading to an increase in the number of ADUs in cities like San Francisco, Oakland, Santa Barbara, and especially L.A. Portland, Oregon, and Austin, Texas, are also known to be very welcoming of ADUs.[53]

Facing the need for affordable housing, it is important to be aware that there are many existing homes that included potential ADUs, if only legislature changed to be more favorable. The city of Durango, Colorado, close to the Mexican border, is an excellent example of a successful program of reform regarding ADUs.[54] Durango changed its land use and development code. It established an accepted process and certain standards for constructing ADUs, limiting the number of individuals who can live in them, establishing the minimum size of the ADU, requiring the owner to actually live in the home, prohibiting the ADU to be rented for vacations, and providing design instructions.

Then, the city also came up with a plan to deal with the ADUs that were already in existence, in essence granting the illegal ones a kind of "amnesty." Planners had to deal with much opposition from citizens who were worried that their neighborhoods would turn into "slums." Ultimately, planners stuck to their guns, highlighting the many benefits of ADUs and making only very minor alterations to the program.[55]

Figure 5. Accessory dwelling units (ADUs) benefit individuals and families who need affordable housing, and they lessen the burden of housing on local infrastructure and the environment.[56]

There are numerous benefits of ADUs, not just for cities and individuals in need of housing, but also for the environment. ADUs make it possible for people to remain flexible regarding their housing situations. For example, an individual could move into the ADU himself or herself and rent out the primary housing, thus being able to save money and remain in the same location. ADUs are also great for housing grown children, aging parents, or care-givers. ADUs are environmentally friendly because they are small, requiring less gas and electricity. Moreover, they are often located in areas that make it possible for individuals to travel on foot or by bike. The per capita residential footprint can also be reduced by ADUs. Finally, ADUs do not have a big impact on the infrastructure of a city.[57]

Mobile Living

I'm suggesting we invest in and promote more mobile living opportunities as a solution to the housing shortage. It's a growing category, fits the model of our leisure culture, and may be a good short-term solution for retirees and young families. There already are many possibilities: rest areas with plug ins, expansion of allowable RV parking lots, and national parks. If you travel the interstates, you get the sense of the sheer number of people already living mobile. Over the road, truck drivers sleep in their cabs by the hundreds of thousands. Similar to tiny home living, there are a great number of Americans that would choose a mobile lifestyle for the short term of one to three years. Many parking lots already provide electric car plug ins; we could improve the system by adding a number of mobile living plug ins. Rest areas and truck stops already have showers and facilities. Wal-Mart also allows overnight parking for free.

When I say mobile living, I'm talking about a non-permanent state of living in general. It's not for everyone, but many are taking on this lifestyle, young and old. This solution is a way to "free up" living space by renting out, or allowing family to reside in your residence for a year or two so they save for a down payment to purchase a place of their own.

The problem with mobile communities is disconnection between our thinking and our laws. In most of the country, you are not allowed to sleep in your car on the side of the road. However, I believe that mobile living can thrive if given a chance, and the times are changing. Sleeping in cars has been made legal in parts of California, where there are now many people legally sleeping in mobile RVs, vans, and SUVs.[58] This is an example of the extreme need for affordable places to live in some cities.

Millions of people today live mobile by choice. You can live on a cruise ship for about $35,000 per year. You eat their food, you travel, they make your room for you, all included—that's mobile living. Living in RVs or "retrofit SUVs," while by no means being the only option for mobile living, could be a fun way to live and save money for a few years. Living in cars while saving money for a down payment is becoming more common.[59]

To make mobile communities happen, we have to further the development of electric plug-ins. Tiny homes of less than 200 square feet, parked on retail properties, could solve the problem of housing for retail workers. Tiny homes run on average 125 to 175 square feet. A modern "prefab" home is around 400 to 500 square feet. A "small home" is around 1,000 square feet.[60] Living in a tiny home is a temporary solution to unlock the market of starter homes and restart the cycle. It could be done quickly—within twenty-four months.

To be clear, I think tiny homes should stay mobile and not become mobile-caravan parks. Many property owners should consider adding some type of additional, sperate living space. Tiny homes should be mobile because it is not advisable to develop a stagnant society dwelling in tiny homes. If the village becomes permanent, it is better to build starter homes.

The mobile community must be accessible and acceptable socially. I am not talking about people just living in their cars like they do in Apple's corporate HQ parking garage, but about people joining the Peace Corps for the year, deciding to sell their houses and live mobile, or—for retired people—traveling abroad and relocating to be near their grandkids. This requires radical shifts of baby boomer mindsets.

Airbnb and VRBO have reduced the need for homeowners to live in one place year-round. Mobile living can be luxurious if you can afford to travel, enjoying the best weather or events all over the U.S.—or the world! Not only do you find corporations offering mobile living solutions, but you have new businesses models in which individuals have bought three or four homes, removing them from the market, and made them dailies.

Allow me to give you a few suggestions for living mobile for a year or longer, in addition to the obvious choices of RV, Airbnb, hotel, or vacation rentals.

Consider teaching English abroad. There are many opportunities to teach English in countries like South Korea, Japan, or Thailand, and many of these teaching opportunities do not even require you to be certified. You could also work in a resort in a foreign country.

Another interesting area of employment that might allow you to live mobile is online freelance work. Whatever your area of expertise may be, check out websites that aim to connect freelancers with potential employers. In certain fields of employment, you may also be able to keep your current job and work remotely.[61]

If you need some money to support your travels to exciting locations, consider travel blogging. Of course, you could start a blog with any sort of focus to make some cash. Also consider housesitting: staying at someone's house for free while looking after it is a great opportunity to save on rent and utilities, although you will probably need a source of income for other expenses.

In other countries, a mobile lifestyle is much more common. For example, in Israel, a young person has to join the military for two years. I am not suggesting that the United States should adopt that model. However, I would like to suggest to millennials to consider whether they would do something hard or inconvenient for a year or two to ultimately achieve their goals. If they could, would they sacrifice living in a small dwelling for twelve to eighteen months to accelerate their student debt payments and to ultimately have their American dream?

I've mentioned we are sometimes tethered to house, even when we don't want to be. Certainly, many people will choose to age in a place, facing the workload and consequences of ongoing property upkeep.

Mobile living, while it is inexpensive and therefore may be a viable solution for those who have faced bankruptcy, is strenuous for individuals above 65 who travel the country in search of seasonal jobs that are physically challenging and low paying.

Nonetheless, there is a very freeing aspect to getting rid of one's home, the most expensive among one's assets. There are certainly various benefits to not owning a home in retirement, including reasons such as having access to the money formerly tied up in real estate, needing to pay off debt, not worrying about maintaining the property, not having to pay land transfer taxes and real estate commissions, preferring the flexibility of renting, moving quickly, and travelling, diversifying one's assets, and experiencing new living situations.[62]

All Hands on Deck

The housing shortage will require the participation of every element of American society, which is only appropriate, given that everyone will be affected if the situation doesn't improve. For too long, we've been content to ignore the problem or simply shrug our shoulders, waiting for someone else to solve it. Now we've reached the point where everyone will need to pitch in—even if that means making sacrifices that may seem uncomfortable. No solution to increasing the supply of affordable housing options can happen without a concerted effort. Public and private citizens need to reevaluate why we sometimes oppose change without looking at the consequences of inaction.

I firmly believe that the housing solutions I have addressed in this chapter, if they were followed, would drastically improve our situation. Baby boomers need to sell their properties and move into housing that fits their current needs. We also need to create more ADUs and pursue more favorable zoning laws. Finally, while it may not be an option for everyone, it is important to explore and encourage the possibility of mobile living.

Chapter Four Questions

Question: In what conditions would you be willing to live for a year or two if it meant you could have enough saved for a down payment? How can you shift your own thinking or expectation of what a "home" looks like? Would you be willing to save, reduce debt, or live differently for a year to be able to afford your first home?

_____

_____

_____

_____

_____

_____

_____

_____

_____

Question: What are some of the potential advantages to baby boomers of downsizing from large homes, even if those home are paid for?

_____

_____

_____

_____

_____

_____

_____

_____

_____

_____

Question: What are the laws regarding ADUs in the area you live in? Have you ever thought about creating an ADU on your property?

_____

_____

_____

_____

_____

_____

_____

_____

_____

_____

_____

Question: How could housing situations like mobile living that typically have a bad reputation be made more desirable and mainstream for the middle class?

_____

_____

_____

_____

_____

_____

_____

_____

_____

_____

Action: Interview a few people who have embraced a minimalist or tiny house philosophy. What have been the greatest advantages and disadvantages to this lifestyle? What would they recommend to those interested in pursuing it?

CHAPTER FIVE

Higher Calling for Higher Education

If we're going to talk about the housing crisis among millennials, then we simply must talk about higher education and its role in this massive nationwide problem.

A college education is now seen as a prerequisite for achieving the American Dream. Poor and working-class parents stress the importance of a four-year degree to their children, even though paying for it has become downright impossible. Indeed, even for middle-class families, rising tuition costs are now unaffordable without substantial student loans.

Government aid is set up to alleviate the burden on the poorest students, while the middle class is left out in the cold. While the very poor get help and the very rich can afford their student loan bills, the middle class sits with little to no aid, making college an even greater burden on an already-burdened group.

In the end, the upper class is the only class who can

reasonably afford higher education. Though the poor receive aid, they are still stuck with some loans that they must figure out without a financially sound home support system. And the middle class is usually left with tens of thousands of dollars in debt—a huge hurdle for a class of people who don't have much excess after they have budgeted for living expenses, retirement, and more.

Quite simply, colleges are failing their students. That formative four-year experience, the very thing intended to prepare young adults for the real world, is now crippling their chances for future success. (And thanks to their college English lit classes, they can grasp the irony of this situation.)

Since colleges and universities are usually responsible for tuition increases, they need to solve this problem for themselves. The good news is, they have the means at their disposal, if they choose to use them.

Radical Solution #6
Endowment-Sponsored Housing

Under the best of circumstances, as we have already discussed, rental prices are prohibitively expensive for young adults just starting out in the working world. But the problem is exacerbated by the rising costs of college tuition. As tuitions rise beyond the scope of what most parents or students can afford, students are being forced to turn to loans to cover costs.

Student loan balances have jumped 150 percent in the last ten years[63] while the starting salary has increased by only 14 percent, according to the executive search firm

Korn Ferry.[64] In total, young adults carry more than $1.4 trillion in college debt.[65] This type of debt was not as prevalent thirty years ago,[66] but it now totals more than all credit card debt combined.[67]

The problem has several layers. First, student loan debt works against a person's debt ratio, which is one of the factors that determines credit rating. Young people generally have lower credit because they've had less time to build a history.

Imagine an outstanding student loan debt of $34,000—which is actually below the national average. Let's assume a monthly payment of $600. If you are making $3,000 a month after taxes—no sure thing—then your loan payment is twenty percent of your pay. That's twenty percent that automatically goes toward debt every single month.

Of course, these number hide a more obvious truth—young college graduates can barely afford an apartment, never mind a home. At $3,000 a month, with a loan payment of $600, there is $2,400 left over to cover every other expense. If you were to take that $2,400 and apply the one-third rule to figure your housing budget, then that puts you in the market for a place that will cost $800. Good luck finding that in most metropolitan cities in the U.S.

College graduates won't be able to dig themselves out of this hole, nor should they, since it was caused by factors outside their control. But their alma maters can—and should—help.

Colleges and universities hold the solution in their endowments.

As of 2016, roughly eight hundred U.S. universities

had a combined $515 billion in endowment assets, as reported by Bloomberg.[68] The *median* U.S. college endowment among ranked institutions in 2017 was $57.5 million.[69]

Unfortunately, due to the nature of endowments and the expectation on the school to grow each donation, much is either being held captive by donor demands or it's being invested in big business to bring about the promised—and required—rate of growth.

But, as CNN Money pointed out, though some good is being done with endowment money, all higher education institutions play a role in *how* they request and raise money for endowments. By making a few simple changes up front, colleges can present solutions to the housing crisis.[70]

Instead of encouraging donors to set up endowments for athletics or building funds, schools could focus on housing solutions. Imagine what a large endowment could do if it were entirely set aside to acquire, build, and maintain reasonable housing. This housing could be rented within the community, thus serving as an investment for the schools, while nearly half of the units would be reserved for a "Launch Program."

Under this plan, alumni or some struggling students—e.g., those who are transitioning into a post-degree career, those who have returned to school, etc.—would pay, for example, $600 in rent. But instead of that sum going directly into rent, $100 would be used for the management of the property, and $500 would go toward rapidly reducing the student's education loans. Students could also pay more toward the loans independently, resulting in even faster repayment.

Using this plan, colleges and universities would have the resources to reduce the burden of student debt and benefit the surrounding community without lowering the return on their investment. The investment in real estate should, could, and would create the same payback.

Of course, this plan will meet some resistance, the strongest of which will be from the colleges themselves. They would need to go back to owning land and buildings as they used to. However, that action would force developers to build more in the market, which then would create lower prices throughout the community through increased supply. In other words, by helping their own, colleges would also be reducing the universal housing shortage.

The Front of the Class

What may ultimately compel colleges to act is the plight of their students and alumni. Helping to reduce the student loan burden and set students up for success within the housing market would have a tangible effect on graduates. It would send the message that colleges care for their own and that institutions are not blind to the struggles that so many face. As schools are forced to compete for students, this sort of goodwill can pay dividends. Endowment-sponsored housing is a solution that not only would put the school in a favorable light but could also lead to positive ripple effects in surrounding communities.

I'm asking millennials to speak up regarding their student debt and its effect on homeownership. We need to go back to our universities and ask them to use endowment dollars to purchase apartment communities—a two-year plan for rapid repayment of loans can unlock more young homeowners.

Debt from student loans is a major obstacle to home-ownership. A study published by *Apartment List* shows that eighty-nine percent of millennials would like to own a home but are unable to purchase one due to student debt. In fact, forty-eight percent of the 6,400 renters surveyed have no money put away towards a down payment.[71] The Federal Reserve Board of Washington, D.C., has identified increases in student debt as a significant cause of lower rates of homeownership.[72]

There are numerous specific financial challenges faced by individuals with significant student loan debt who would like to own homes. The first challenge is those in-dividuals' "debt-to-income ratio," which causes them to be denied when they apply for mortgages. The second ob-stacle is their low credit scores, in some cases caused by defaulting on student loans. Third, as I have discussed above, individuals who have student debt have a not able to save for a down payment.

There are significant housing issues created by high college tuition and immense student loan debt. As I've suggested in this chapter, an attractive solution to these problems is endowment-sponsored housing, where uni-versities would focus on guiding donors toward housing solutions, purchasing apartment communities, and then creating a "launch program." A large portion of the rent payments of individuals who are part of the program would go towards paying off their educational debt, which would benefit the students, the community, and ultimately, the university.

Millennials need to go back to their universities and speak up regarding the crippling effects of student loans, pushing for this all-around beneficial solution. With the strategic use of temporary housing solutions like employer housing, ADUs, and college endowment programs, millennials can save money while permanent starter-home developments are built. This will allow them to set aside the funds they'll need for a down payment—so they can finally buy their first home.

Chapter Five Questions

Question: What are some ways that students can go to college without accumulating massive debt? What types of college programs make it possible to get a traditional degree without needing to acquire student loans?

_____

_____

_____

_____

_____

_____

_____

_____

_____

_____

Question: What financial challenges is a student with high student loan debt left with? In what ways does student debt affect that student's ability to purchase a home?

_____

_____

_____

_____

_____

_____

_____

_____

_____

_____

_____

Question: How would endowment-sponsored housing be beneficial to colleges as well as indebted alumni?

_____

_____

_____

_____

_____

_____

_____

_____

_____

_____

_____

_____

Action: Identify influential alumni of your college or university. Connect with them about working together to develop interest in endowment-sponsored housing.

CHAPTER SIX

Movers, Shakers, and Builders

Whenever a huge problem arises, people naturally want to start assigning blame. A ten-million-roof housing shortage? Sprawling high-end suburban homes on the cusp of massive devaluation? These problems have to be someone's fault. On the surface, just who that *someone* is seems obvious—the developers. They're the ones, after all, not building enough homes or, at the very least, building the wrong kinds.

Turns out, the developers are the good guys. If we get out of their way, they can help ease the housing crisis.

Radical Solution #7
Freedom for Developers

Local developers often get a bad rap. Though they are mischaracterized as greedy corner-cutters looking out for their own bottom line, most of them have a genuine desire to improve their cities and towns. They understand how a beautiful building or well-designed neighborhood can foster a sense of pride and identity in a community. Most local developers, if left to their own devices, would do a fantastic job.

But rarely, if ever, are they left to their own devices. First and foremost, developers are held hostage to the whims and desires of the market. To remain successful, they must build the homes that consumers want to buy. And, as we discussed, what many consumers had grown to desire is *more of everything*. More rooms, more square-footage, and more luxurious, exotic features. Once one new home is built with an in-ground pool, they all must have them. Then a jacuzzi, a pergola, a multi-level deck, and it goes on and on. At the present rate, a koi pond—stocked seasonally—will soon become a standard feature in suburban homes.

This desire for ever-larger homes has led to the much-maligned suburban sprawl of many metropolitan areas. Suburban developments farther and farther away from downtown districts are built; these unsustainable communities increase traffic and commute times for workers. Yet these homes further out *still* aren't affordable to most buyers, especially younger ones, thanks to the housing shortage and cost of the construction of the homes.

But what if consumer thinking changed? What if the general public, now cognizant of the reality of the housing crisis, looked to developers as people with solutions rather than people who can throw together a dream home in less than a year?

Well, then we face new challenges.

For one, we have fewer skilled builders than ever before. In fact, the National Builders Association has half the number of builders than it did a decade ago. This, in large part, is a lingering aftershock of the 2008 recession. Many builders were forced out of the business, due to the steep decline in home construction, while aspiring developers were scared into other industries by the uncertainty and alarming daily headlines in newspapers and online.[73]

The education system itself bears some responsibility for the lack of skilled builders. It prizes four-year degrees and service-based careers over tech certificates and trade-based careers. This reduces the number of apprentices looking to get into the construction industry and working under skilled master builders.[74]

It's not just qualified developers we lack. We're also running out of space. Years of sprawling satellite communities in places like Atlanta have reduced the amount of room available to build new starter homes. Our big, new houses sit on even bigger lots. Topographical limitations in places like Asheville, North Carolina, have much the same effect. We have taken what land we have, and we've built ten houses when we could have built thirty or forty.

Developers face numerous obstacles and have to jump through many hoops to get approval for housing, which causes the entire process to take much longer than necessary. Let's examine the long list of stakeholders in this process. Each person or group represents an oftentimes unique component to either the problem or the solution to the housing crisis. Similar to the housing crash and the following Great Recession, there is plenty of blame or praise to go around, depending on your perspective.

Picture this incomplete list as a funnel, or meat grinder—whichever mental picture suits—with the output being a housing unit, or multiple multi housing unit communities.

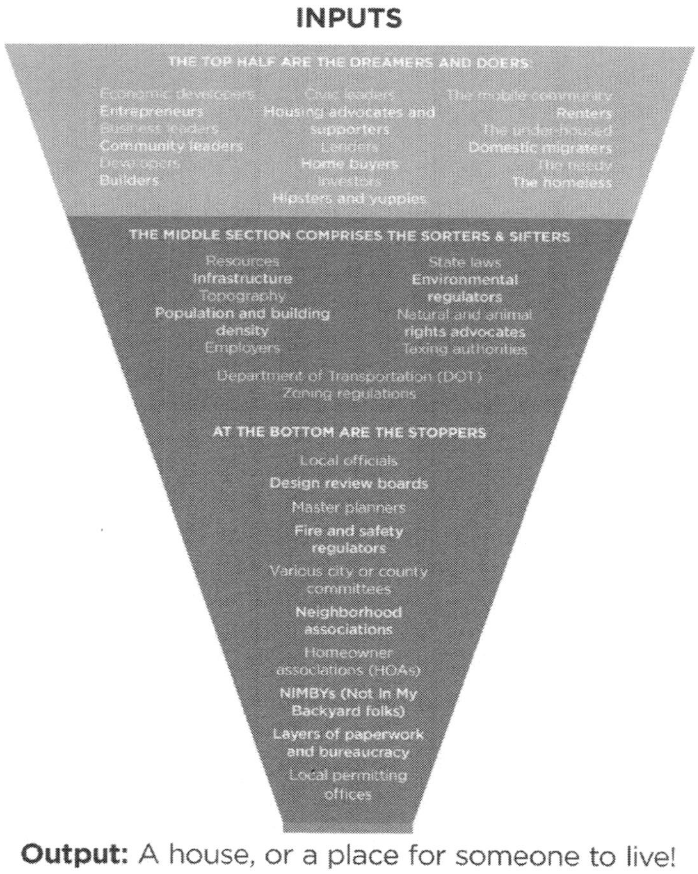

INPUTS

THE TOP HALF ARE THE DREAMERS AND DOERS

Economic developers • Civic leaders • The mobile community
Entrepreneurs • Housing advocates and • Renters
Business leaders • supporters • The under-housed
Community leaders • Lenders • Domestic migraters
Developers • Home buyers • The needy
Builders • Investors • The homeless
Hipsters and yuppies

THE MIDDLE SECTION COMPRISES THE SORTERS & SIFTERS

Resources • State laws
Infrastructure • Environmental
Topography • regulators
Population and building • Natural and animal
density • rights advocates
Employers • Taxing authorities
Department of Transportation (DOT)
Zoning regulations

AT THE BOTTOM ARE THE STOPPERS

Local officials
Design review boards
Master planners
Fire and safety
regulators
Various city or county
committees
Neighborhood
associations
Homeowner
associations (HOAs)
NIMBYs (Not In My
Backyard folks)
Layers of paperwork
and bureaucracy
Local permitting
offices

Output: A house, or a place for someone to live!

Figure 6. The housing funnel: inputs and outputs.

Although local developers face many challenges, we

can rely on them to innovate *if* we allow them to. They take great pride—and, frankly, profit—in their ability to deliver what the market requires. In other words, if we ask them to build communities of densely-packed, affordable starter homes, they'll find a way. But we need to change our mindset and accept the fact that giant homes on spacious, private lots within sprawling neighborhoods are not helping the situation. They're suffocating it.

Let the developers develop. Let them work with urban planners to find the best way to maximize space. And let's find a way to cater to our growing group of millennials near urban cores who need starter homes, rather than only focusing on the upper classes who we think still want mini mansions on mini estates.

Radical Solution #8
Tax Incentives

We've mentioned the dangers of NIMBY (Not In My Back Yard) and how it affects potential tenants in retail conversions, but it's worth discussing here as well. Local homeowners—who form neighborhoods, which form communities—are often the biggest "obstacles" when it comes to changes in development strategies. In truth, they tend to oppose changes of any kind at all. Often, this resistance is masked disingenuously as practical concerns over falling property values.

Community groups push to enforce or even add rules and regulations whenever a new development is broached. The idea of something as mundane as widening a road will be met with consternation. And even one loud, angry voter can be enough to send local officials into fits of paralysis. In this way, new construction is contested, permits are delayed, and the flawed status quo continues to win the day.

To be clear, homeowners are citizens with civic rights. They deserve to be heard. But it's also true that politicians and neighborhood associations need to do a better job of facing down resistance with re-education and in some cases, fortitude they often lack. The fact is, when community members cling stubbornly to old-fashioned ideas and principles, they fail to grasp that they're unwittingly arguing on behalf of leaving major problems unsolved.

Local and county authorities can take proactive action to help prospective homebuyers. Specifically, they need to re-examine property tax laws.

Property taxes are overwhelming in some states. People moving to a new area can have taxes three times higher than longer-term residents on the same street. There is also very little continuity in property tax valuation. Even people who can afford escalating home prices are often scared off by the thought of getting into a situation that causes them to be a victim to the whim of the assessor and market. This only increases housing immobility problems, as people choose to stay put and face "the devil they know" rather than strike out and face "the devil they don't."

Property taxes account for a large percentage of rental expense, for every renter in America. Whether we believe it or not, the renter bears the expense of property tax. As an owner of rental property, and a veteran broker of multifamily assets, I can tell you that a portion of the amount of rent someone pays goes mostly to offset the cost of the property tax. Furthermore, it is almost a dollar for dollar offset. So, if one rental home has an "old" assessment of, say, $1,200 per year, the first $100 of monthly rent collected goes to property tax.

The same is true if, down the same street, another home has a property tax bill of $2,400. The rent someone pays is almost certainly $100 more per month to the tenant. It's the business of renting to cover *all* your expenses as an owner, such as taxes, insurance, repairs, etc. and to make a profit at the end of the year. In defense of owners, sometimes you go through the headache of renting all year and one thing or the other, expense wise, is the difference between a profit and a loss.

An example of this is covered in Mathew Desmond's excellent book entitled *Evicted.* The early chapters tell the story of an owner who struggles to keep tenants housed within their means, only to fight a system of authority that undermines the very goal of affordability.

Property taxes are necessary, of course, but they are burdensome nonetheless. One could suggest that property taxes are highly regressive in nature, because the lower-income rental residents shoulder much of the burden. In addition, our struggling millennials have the same plight, only worse! They are living in the newly built or upgraded apartments, with student debt, and in a property with perhaps a significantly higher tax burden per unit. Worse still is the reality that many millennial require much less in the way of county services. For example, those who do not have children yet do not require the school system. Since the largest portion of most property taxes go to fund the schools, millennials pay for area homeowners' children to go to K–12 while many millennials themselves may not have school-aged children yet. I'm pointing this out to encourage millennials: make some noise! You need a renter tax credit to go toward a down payment of your own home.

There are some programs out there, but my hope is to:

1. Educate individuals that property tax for renters is a huge burden.

2. Encourage local governing bodies to look for ways to help renters become homeowners in their communities.

3. Clearly articulate that one of the biggest reasons affordability is out of control is supply, but right behind that is property tax burden, which as I've pointed out, is shouldered by the renter.

This leads us to our radical solution: counties need to be courting renters with renter tax rebates—specifically, for buying a home in the same county or state. Experts on the reduction of poverty have been suggesting the implementation of a refundable tax credit for renters in areas with high rental costs. The results of such an approach would be significant. Simulations show that almost sixty percent of poor renters would benefit from the credit, as would over seventy percent of renters who face the burden of extremely high housing costs. The average credit amount would be $2,059. Among those who would receive the credit, the poverty rate would go down by 12.4

percent. Moreover, the deep poverty rate would be reduced by 8.8 percent. Among the individuals who continue being poor, the poverty gap is reduced by almost one third. The cost would be $24.1 billion annually.[75]

Renters are ultimately paying the property tax for the owners. Property taxes keep rising, and that annual expense is simply divided by the number of units in a building—which leads to rent increases. In my state, the average property tax bill on an apartment building is nearly $1,800 per year, or $150 per month. So, if your rent is $1,000 for a two-bedroom apartment, the first fifteen percent goes to pay property taxes!

A targeted renter property tax rebate will create lower overall rent and incentivize millennials to stay within the community. Another incentive could be a deduction from future taxes to the level of paid property tax during a renting period. Additionally, communities could choose to temporarily lower the property taxes of all homes within a certain area should that area open to starter-home developers. A program aimed at keeping renters in your community is a property tax rebate. Local taxing bodies should consider applying a portion of a rental properties' taxes into a rebate to help these renters become homeowners.

There are a number of paths that can be taken when we start to consider how city and county governments can step in to alleviate the problem—these ideas are only scratching the surface. Again, let's look at other cities that have implemented strategies and copy the best practices nationwide. By getting our city councils and local politicians talking about the problem, we will inevitably have a number of communities each trying a variety of solutions and then sharing their findings with the rest of the nation. It could be the jump-start we need.

Radical Solution #9
People First, Then Businesses

Huge, popular employers like Google and Apple employ thousands at their central bases of operations, providing an incredible boost to local economies. For this reason, states are desperate to attract their business. But it's no coincidence that these headquarters are usually located in extraordinarily expensive housing markets. In fact, the big tech companies' presence *drives up the housing markets* by increasing the need—and often pushing other types of lower-earning workers out. If we examine this cause and effect scenario between employer and the housing market more closely, we'll see that it actually provides a unique opportunity to combat our current shortage.

First, let's look at how states woo corporations. Consider Amazon's recent search for their second headquarters. States, cities, and towns across the country, of course, competed for this opportunity, providing a variety of incentives—tax breaks—as a wooing tactic. That practice makes complete sense—the addition of an employer of that size is, quite literally, a transformational possibility for a given community.

But of the over two hundred cities who entered the Amazon HQ competition, twenty were considered top bids. Only two localities—one in New York City and the other in Northern Virginia[76]—were ultimately selected (at least, until political controversy led Amazon to de-select New York[77]).

Selection as a headquarters will no doubt provide a significant boost to the local economy in Arlington, Virginia. However, it will quite likely drive the already expensive Northern Virginia housing market to new heights of unaffordability for most people. The local governments win, Amazon wins, and current landlords and property owners win (big), but renters suffer. Even making comparatively high salaries, workers and residents will be squeezed by the runaway train that is the local housing market.

Eventually, this market may begin to negatively impact Amazon itself. The company will have to increase wages significantly to attract workers—or consider alternatives like building housing for them—thus impacting its bottom line.

Now let's turn our attention to the over two hundred communities that were outbid for Amazon's shiny new headquarters. What happened to all the money and incentives the other places offered?

Well, in the strictest sense of the word, that money never really existed. Those incentives were really lost revenue in taxes that the state or local governments were willing to sacrifice as an investment of sorts. The addition of an employer the size of Amazon is, quite literally, a transformational possibility for the local and larger economy. Every locality hoped that the tax breaks they offered a huge corporation to relocate would be paid back tenfold thanks to the money that Amazon—and its thousands of workers—would infuse into the community.

This dusty old model of providing incentives to attract employers operates on a principle memorably para-phrased in the classic movie *Field of Dreams*: "If you build it, they will come." Workers, according to this idea, follow companies.

But this simply doesn't hold true anymore. In 2018, es-pecially in tech or web-based industries, an employee's physical presence isn't required at an office every day. Progressive companies are already re-thinking the very nature of work with concepts like remote staff, teleconfer-ences, and virtual meetings. A person can work for a huge tech company in Hong Kong while living comfortably in Denver, Colorado, without any drop in efficiency or productivity.

So, what does this all mean? Quite simply, we don't need to attract Amazon to grow a vibrant, financially sus-tainable community in 2018. We merely need to attract the workers that Amazon needs.

In other words, it's time for states to re-imagine, "If you build it, they will come." Instead of focusing on bringing in big business, focus on housing. *Build* afforda-ble housing communities full of able young workers, and *they*—big, labor-starved companies—will come. This ef-fort can be funded by the tax breaks and incentives that would have gone to corporations such as Amazon. It can be considered a "consolation prize" of sorts. Your city may not win over Amazon, but you can win at housing.

Block by Block

Forward thinking and *innovative* aren't words we typically use to describe governments. But those qualities—and plenty more—will be required to dig America out of the hole that is the housing shortage. That being said, we don't need to reinvent the wheel. Many of the solutions that can ease our current crisis require only the courage to re-think practices and institutions already in place.

If we demand more of our leaders, if we present ideas and solutions and push for action, then we can begin to mobilize our towns, cities, and counties to take care of this massive issue, one city block and country acre at a time.

WORKBOOK

Chapter Six Questions

Question: What is your attitude toward developers? How can we give them the freedom they need to create the buildings we need?

_____

_____

_____

_____

_____

_____

_____

_____

_____

_____

_____

Question: How can local governments restructure property taxes to help encourage homeownership and, especially, first-time homebuyers?

_____

_____

_____

_____

_____

_____

_____

_____

_____

_____

_____

Question: Imagine a city that focused on attracting workers versus attracting businesses. What amenities besides affordable housing would incentivize workers to move there? What businesses would grow through an influx of young workers and families?

_____

_____

_____

_____

_____

_____

_____

_____

_____

_____

_____

_____

Action: Interview an influential local developer and converse about the concepts in this book. What innovative ideas does the developer have, and how have those ideas been received by local leaders?

CHAPTER SEVEN

We Need Uncle Sam

Government intervention in the housing market has been a controversial subject for a long time, as some past interventions have been successful while others have done serious damage. There are certainly pros, but also cons, to government intervention. Let's explore if there are some positive ways in which Uncle Sam can help solve the present housing crisis when it comes to closing and repurposing unnecessary military installations, saving the U.S. Department of Housing and Urban Development (HUD), 40-year mortgages, and executive orders.

Radical Solution #10
Military Bases

As needs—and threats—evolve, the United States military is constantly re-aligning resources throughout the world. These changes often create redundancies and inefficiencies, some of which can be quite expensive. One way the Pentagon monitors and reduces these expenses is the Base Realignment and Closure (BRAC) commission. As its name suggests, BRAC studies and recommends to Congress a number of military installations that can be consolidated or closed to save the government money. The lion's share of savings comes from closures, since operating these bases is enormously expensive.

Four rounds of base closures in the 1990s resulted in $7 billion in savings yearly, according to Mackenzie Eaglen, a resident fellow at the Marilyn Ware Center for Security Studies at the American Enterprise Institute.[78] A fifth round of closures in 2005 tacked on another $4 billion in savings annually—though it had actually cost the government $35 billion to implement this fifth round of closures. Even factoring in that expensive debacle, we've saved more than $140 billion this century.

These closings don't indicate a loss of military strength. Rather, they are recommended as a result of internal changes that create redundancies in the more than eight hundred military bases across the country and the 800,000 employees working there.

Creating a more efficient military and saving billions in taxpayer dollars seems like a no-brainer. Yet a new round of proposed closures in 2021 will likely not receive Congressional approval. For one thing, base closures tend to be very unpopular with certain voter blocks, particularly Republicans, who pride themselves on being pro-military. Such voters may consider closing bases a sure sign of the armed forces being weakened.

Others worry about the economic impact of a base closure on the local community, though it should be noted that communities often find creative solutions in these instances. Consider the Philadelphia Navy Yard, a base founded in 1776 and closed in 1995. Roughly seven thousand jobs were lost at the time. Then the city of Philadelphia redeveloped the port and opened it to a variety of companies, including national retail chains and restaurants. More than 11,000 people now work at the naval yard.[79]

So, why can't we close several unnecessary—and expensive—military installations and convert them into housing? Like closed retail spaces, they already have all the infrastructure they need, so the cost of the conversion, if well managed, would not be prohibitive. Environmental concerns like asbestos and possible chemical pollution would need to be thoroughly vetted, of course.

The positive effect on the housing shortage would be incalculable. California, for example, has 3,800,000 acres of military bases—and one of the biggest housing crunches in the country.[80] Many of the 38 million people living there can't afford a half-acre of undeveloped land, much less a home. Up to about forty apartment-style units can easily be built on one acre, so a forty-acre base would mean 1,600 additional homes. Even in a worst-case scenario, the existing base barracks, which often houses military personnel and their families, could be utilized.

This idea is not without precedent. In 1995, a Navy recruiting center in Orlando, Florida, was closed and redeveloped as Baldwin Park, a now-thriving neighborhood of homes, schools, and stores. The only thing this community lacks is affordability, as I can personally attest after living in the vicinity in the late '90s and early 2000s.

Rather than create reasonably-sized single-family homes, the developers followed the same trends that have partially led to our current crisis—sprawling, luxury housing beyond the financial reach of most homebuyers.[81] A similar scenario played out in San Diego, when a 361-acre navy recruitment center closed in 1997 was born again as Liberty Station, a popular mixed-use development.

In the case of base closures, we have opportunity, universal benefit, and successful test cases—all that's required is the necessary will to transform these bases into living spaces. This would begin with educating nervous constituents about the benefits—rather than drawbacks—to local economies, of which several examples can serve as a case-in-point. Harder to navigate would be the political party divide, particularly in this day and age, where reason and sense are sacrificed for party-centric talking points (e.g., "Vote NO to closing bases if you support our troops!") But when even the Pentagon itself actively advocates for BRAC recommendations on the basis of cost-savings, it seems possible to bridge these divides.

State	Acres of Military Bases	Military Bases as % of State
California	3,838,554	3.85%
Arizona	3,583,066	4.93%
New Mexico	3,643,513	4.69%
Nevada	3,532,126	5.03%
Utah	1,814,893	3.45%
North Carolina	1,704,623	5.48%
Washington	942,457	2.22%

Florida	690,867	2.01%
Texas	495,002	0.30%
Alaska	462,936	0.13%
Virginia	439,596	1.74%
Colorado	240,186	0.36%
Louisiana	234,695	0.85%
Hawaii	230,280	5.60%
Oklahoma	190,359	0.43%
Mississippi	174,864	0.58%
Kentucky	168,313	0.67%
Indiana	158,977	0.69%
Tennessee	142,702	0.54%
Kansas	139,166	0.27%
Idaho	136,455	0.26%
Alabama	132,437	0.41%
Oregon	131,255	0.21%
Maryland	109,301	1.76%
Georgia	98,752	0.27%
Arkansas	85,729	0.26%
New Jersey	71,512	1.52%
Montana	61,708	0.07%
South Carolina	59,129	0.31%
Iowa	50,684	0.14%
Pennsylvania	43,144	0.15%
Ohio	34,880	0.13%
North Dakota	34,654	0.08%
Wyoming	31,967	0.05%
Missouri	29,187	0.07%
New York	26,870	0.09%
Massachusetts	24,665	0.49%
Maine	21,988	0.11%
Nebraska	20,195	0.04%
Illinois	18,817	0.05%
Wisconsin	14,500	0.04%
Michigan	13,533	0.04%
Vermont	11,382	0.19%
South Dakota	9,694	0.02%
Delaware	4,118	0.33%
West Virginia	3,637	0.02%
New Hampshire	3,118	0.05%
Rhode Island	2,895	0.44%

Minnesota	2,888	0.01%
Connecticut	1,670	0.05%
District of Columbia	1,559	3.99%

Figure 7. The amount of land (acres and percentage) taken up by military bases in each state as of 2014.[82]

The chart above shows the total acreage consumed by military bases in the U.S. as of 2014. The state of California, for example, has over 3.8 million acres of military bases for about 38 million residents—and a house can be built on one-tenth of an acre. In short, California military bases encompass enough land (hypothetically) to grant every resident sufficient space for a house!

Radical Solution #11
Save HUD and Convert to the Forty-Year Mortgage

The solution of saving the U.S. Department of Housing and Urban Development (HUD) implies the need to return the agency to its mission of providing equal and affordable housing. In the past, HUD took it upon itself to create housing that was government backed. HUD was very active in the 1960s and '70s; unfortunately, its theories had negative implications, and HUD was instrumental in creating the housing bubble.

Because of HUD, too many people became homeowners in the 2000s, ushering in the housing crash. HUD was partially responsible for creating the bubble by backing all of the mortgages that later, essentially, went bad. Moreover, certain segments of the population, including African

Americans and other ethnic minorities, continued to experience lower rates of homeownership.

HUD has recently announced that it plans to change its mission statement, removing a number of references to inclusivity from its website. The new focus appears to be on self-sufficient communities.[83] HUD released a statement on March 7, 2018, claiming to have made only "modest" changes to the mission statement and expressing a continued commitment to providing housing that is inclusive, without discriminating against any Americans. Moreover, the HUD website currently still states that creating "inclusive communities" is a part of its mission.[84]

We must have a nationally recognized "campaign" or effort to restore the American Dream. This means looking at the past successes of our history of housing, such as the G.I. Bill, taking the best practices of that era, and combining them with our knowledge of inclusive communities to promote affordable housing from the top down. If it is communicated from the top down, from President Trump, to HUD, to states, to local communities that affordable housing is a mandate of the highest office, then we can return to our free market economy to provide affordable dwellings.

We simply ask our current president, who is clearly a real estate expert, to exert the power of the office, through the agency of HUD, to promote the original mission of HUD. We encourage him to be the president who brings his private-sector expertise to Washington and uses the pulpit of the presidency to help fix housing. President Trump is the "real estate" president, and we suggest that he may use the remainder of his administration to truly "make America great again" by allowing the free market to house our citizens and restore the American Dream.

In October 2017, the Urban Institute published a report exploring "Trends in Housing Problems and Federal Housing Assistance," focusing on the last ten years. The conclusions of the report highlight the slowing rate of household formation in general and the increase of renter households.[85] Almost two thirds of renter households were also low-income households. The report also concluded that, among renters, affordability problems are increasing, while the problem of housing that is physically inadequate is declining. More than fifty percent of all renters have some kind of housing needs.

Specific to HUD assistance meant to aid low-income households, the report found that there had not been a significant increase in the number of households that received assistance over the last ten years, but there had been an increase in the number of those who received housing vouchers. However, there has been a large increase in need, and the housing gap has become much wider. Increasingly, those benefiting from HUD programs are elderly and differently-abled individuals, and fewer families with children benefit from HUD programs. It looks like the gap in housing assistance will continue to grow worse.[86] [87]

Currently, one of the biggest issues we have is that the debt ratio of the buyers is too high, and the housing cost is too expensive. Therefore, the high cost pushes more people into rent, and the return investment on rentals is zero. We need to create ownership through HUD, so we can reclaim the American Dream.

The 40-Year-Mortgage Concept

The goal of promoting a longer amortized mortgage, meaning a mortgage that is paid off through regular payments over time, is to lower monthly payments. This flexibility helps put families in homes but does slow the paydown of principal. The national average for homeowners moving has traditionally been seven years.

By suggesting and allowing longer amortization loans, we can encourage more ownership with more affordable monthly payments. Our goal is to create more affordable solutions. If we add to the mix a longer-term mortgage, we could have more people qualify for a mortgage when you factor in all their other monthly debt (car loans/student loans).

In fact, perhaps the most beneficial government change to mortgages is to allow borrowers to roll in their student loans. Risky, but since we are already facing high delinquency rates on student loans, something radical must be done!

The 40-year-mortgage takes longer to pay back, but the individual payments are lower. With a 40-year mortgage, the borrower can be more flexible because of the lower individual payments, and the borrower can nonetheless choose to pay off more at a time if he or she is able. Moreover, certain 40-year mortgages can be sold to Fannie Mae.

There is a possibility that Congress will change mortgage regulations in a way that might affect 40-year and other non-standard mortgages, but the details are unclear.

Individuals who own homes and cannot make their regular mortgage payments could benefit from a possible loan modification agreement that would include a change to a 40-year term. This may be beneficial if homeowners can afford this new, modified payment along with their regular expenses.[88]

We now have decades of data to show how long a home can last once it has been built. Extending a mortgage term to a longer period helps affordability, but still gives lenders a comfort level that a structure will still be sound thirty to forty years after it is built.

Executive Orders

The federal government has used executive orders in the past to help all Americans have a roof over their heads. It is time once again to consider using an executive order to mandate accessible and affordable housing for all. The government must return to the basis principal of providing "shelter" at all income levels. I'm suggesting the federal government needs to pay for it, not just free us up to make faster decisions at the local level. We ask earnestly for a new executive order that unites all governing bodies to streamline the approval process for more housing.

Here are a few examples of past housing laws and related executive orders that have been successful:

1. Fair Housing Act (Title VIII of the Civil Rights Act of 1968) protects renters, buyers, and those who seek mortgages or other housing assistance from discrimination on the basis of race,

color, national origin, religious affiliation, sex, family status, and disability.

2. Title VI of the Civil Rights Act of 1964 protects individuals from discrimination based on race, color, or national origin within federally assisted programs or activities.

3. Section 504 of the Rehabilitation Act of 1973 protects individuals from discrimination on the basis of disability within federally assisted programs or activities.

4. Section 109 of Title I of the Housing and Community Development Act of 1974 protects individuals from discrimination based on race, color, national origin, sex, or religious affiliation within any CDBG-funded program or activity

5. Executive Order 11063 mandates an end to segregation in federally funded housing.

6. Executive Order 11246, as amended, mandates an end to discrimination based on race, color, religious affiliation, sex, or national origin in federal employment.

7. Executive Order 12892, as amended, mandates that the programs and activities of federal agencies have to pursue fair housing, coordinated by the Secretary of HUD.[89]

In conclusion, intervention and innovation from the

federal government in the form of closing and repurposing military bases, HUD, 40-year mortgages, and executive orders has the potential to have a positive impact. In the case of redundant military installations, the government would save billions in operating costs and create priceless housing opportunities, for which the necessary infrastructure would already be present. In the same vein, making affordable housing a mandate of the highest office, pursuing a top-down approach via HUD, 40-year mortgages, and relevant executive orders would allow us to create win-win situations and reclaim the American Dream. Let us make an appeal to our government to intervene and make a change for the better in the housing market.

WORKBOOK

Chapter Seven Questions

Question: What is your opinion of government intervention and intentional manipulation of the housing market? What do you see as the advantages and disadvantages? What would you describe as the ideal role of government in regulating housing and mortgages?

_____

_____

_____

_____

_____

_____

_____

_____

_____

Question: What are some advantages of closing unnecessary military installations and converting them into housing?

_____

_____

_____

_____

_____

_____

_____

_____

_____

_____

_____

Question: How can HUD re-examine its role to remain relevant and useful in the new century?

_____

_____

_____

_____

_____

_____

_____

_____

_____

_____

_____

_____

Action: Learn about the history, role, and programs of HUD (hud.gov).

CHAPTER EIGHT

The Future of Housing

The future of housing could turn out to be similar to that of other great industries and trends. This book was written to begin ushering in those changes. Think about how different the retail landscape is today, with online shopping versus mom-and-pop, brick and mortar shops.

The auto industry is in the throes of massive upheaval with the advent of self-driving vehicles. Transportation in general is changing, with hyperloop technology, and private space travel, just to name a few. The sharing economy of rides has already radically changed the taxi and rental car business.

I've been a music fan forever. Electronic and computerized music has changed the rules of rock and roll and for drums and guitars almost overnight. The change to digital music, from recording to consuming, has reshaped that industry—in my opinion, for the better.

I grew up watching cartoons that were made with hand-drawn cells. Now, it's CG (computer generated), and once we got used to it, many of us found we prefer the new way of doing things.

For housing, as I've already suggested, a similar reset is coming. We have built the "low hanging fruit," as the term goes. That is to say, we have built what the banks wanted to lend on, the builders could profit on, and taxing authorities could benefit from: expensive single and multifamily dwellings.

Without a concerted effort to "fix" affordable housing, we potentially doom the largest generation to have ever populated America: the millennials.

As we know, the foundation of capitalism is supply and demand. We have more than enough demand. Now we need supply—lots of it. The trickle-down effect does not work in housing, nor does the big government bottom-up approach of the 1960s. We need the private sector to step up, and local communities to step up, and see the need for radical solutions to our housing dilemma.

In this book, I've proposed that we need a minimum of an additional 10 million units over the next ten years—over and above our average need of and current production of 1.2 million units per year. Moreover, these units must be affordable for the masses, i.e., those working and earning the average salary of the American people. Their rents/mortgage payment must be built to match twenty-eight percent of their pay. We can do this; we must do this, for millennials, future generations, and the American Dream.

Imagine a future of mobility and housing flexibility that looks like the workforce of today. Mere decades ago, hundreds of employees sat in cubicles or corner offices in office buildings. Today's gig economy, where individuals have temporary, flexible, rather than permanent, full-time jobs, runs more on a mobile platform of community workspace, WiFi, and public space—think of individuals working on their laptops at Starbucks. In perhaps the next decade, we will see a large number of people changing the housing concept in similar fashion. Just as transportation is changing so rapidly, from Uber to FlixBus to self-driving cars, we can see a housing ecosystem evolve in a similar manner. For example, Airbnb has individuals living in a shared economy. Home sharing, granny flats, and flexible living arrangements are possibly one click away.

Blockchain is the next frontier of the real estate market, making inroads at a fast clip. Similar to crowdfunding and real estate investment trusts (REITs), blockchain could turn real estate ownership into more fractional ownership. Today, most real estate transactions outside of single-family home purchases are by big investors or corporations. The use of the technology will make it possible to have transparent transactions that sellers and buyers will benefit from. The blockchain essentially makes it possible for parties to conduct financial transactions without the use of a middleman, because it utilizes a large number of computers that keep an identical, encrypted record that can be accessed by anyone.[90]

From real-time ledgers to full-on shared databases and processes, the blockchain throws the doors wide open with possibilities in real estate. Instead of one owner, the blockchain will make a crowdfunding style of transaction possible for property once owned by one family or a few investors. So, in the near future, millennials locked out of real estate will have more options to become owners on a smaller scale.

Brand new, start from scratch communities are another interesting future trend. Age-restricted communities like Del Webb and the Villages in Florida are good examples of master-planned communities that were once in the middle of nowhere.

I'm a big fan of Disney, and the massive Orlando park system, built mostly in the 1970s and '80s, is a model of efficiency. Most states could only dream of building a vast system like Disney. Complete with roads, bridges, lakes, and, of course, a super-cool monorail, Disney built a "city" at a fraction of the cost of today's mass transit.

When you start from scratch, you can do this. I'm guessing our future holds some pretty cool communities with the advent of new technologies like Uber's "flying taxi", where one could commute to a major city center fifty miles away in fifteen to twenty minutes. It's conceivable that some vast swathes of barren land could suddenly become viable locations for serious residential and commercial development.[91]

Additional trends we don't even consider today as an option could someday be common place. My favorite future trend in real estate one day will be the 3D-printed house. I'm not sure when or where this may happen, but ever since my son 3D-printed a gift for me, I can't stop thinking about how we might all be living in multicolored, mini 3D-printed homes. These homes have the potential to be completed much faster and cheaper than is currently the case.

Natural Disasters

As we consider the future of the housing market, we cannot ignore the effects of natural disasters on housing. Rising oceans put millions at risk of losing everything. We can debate the causes of a warming planet all day. What we cannot deny is that millions and millions of homes are within range of a few feet of rising ocean waters.

Let me give you an example of the effects natural disasters can have on housing: over one million units of housing in the Gulf states suffered damage from Hurricane Katrina and the floods that followed it. Fifty percent of the damaged homes were in Louisiana, and seventy percent of occupied housing units in New Orleans were damaged.[92]

Similarly, over 204,000 apartment buildings and homes in Harris County were damaged by Hurricane Harvey. Almost seventy-five percent of these housing units were not within the hundred-year floodplain regulated by the government; therefore, many of the damaged homes and apartment buildings were not prepared to deal with storm damage and flooding, nor were they covered by insurance.[93]

A recent report published by RealtyTrac claims that forty-three percent of housing units in America are either in high or even very high danger of being affected by a natural disaster. The risk is highest in California, where 8.4 million housing units are in danger, followed by Florida, with 6.7 housing units at a high risk. New York City is the city with the greatest risk, with 3.5 million homes in danger, followed by Los Angeles, where 2.5 million homes are at high risk. Another report, released by the Internal Displacement Monitoring Centre, suggests that natural disasters have forced circa 26.4 people annually from their homes since 2008.[94]

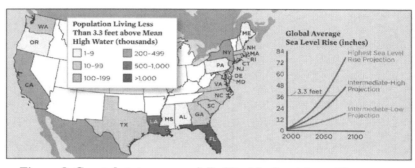

Figure 8. Coastal states—especially Florida, Louisiana, New York, and California—are highly vulnerable to severe flooding and damage from storms and rising sea levels connected to ocean warming. Natural disasters of all kinds can seriously exacerbate housing shortages.[95]

Unforeseen events like fires, earthquakes, or even man-made disasters like bombings or the ravages of war can significantly change the housing landscape. None of us can be sure what the future holds. However, we can attempt to be prepared for catastrophes. Today, start thinking about how you can affect the future of housing. Let's dream big about housing every man, woman, and child affordably. After all, shelter is a basic necessity. It was yesterday, it is today, and it will still be tomorrow.

WORKBOOK

Chapter Eight Questions

Question: In your own words, describe why there is a need for a reset in housing. In what specific areas do you see a need for change?

_____

_____

_____

_____

_____

_____

_____

_____

_____

_____

Question: What new trends and technological developments in housing are you aware of? How can they make a difference in shaping the housing market? Explain why these new technologies excite you, or why they don't.

_____

_____

_____

_____

_____

_____

_____

_____

_____

_____

_____

Question: What are the effects of natural disasters on housing? Can you give a few examples from recent history?

_____

_____

_____

_____

_____

_____

_____

_____

_____

_____

_____

_____

Action: Research 3D-printed houses, the blockchain, and other new housing trends online, keeping track of the most recent developments.

CONCLUSION

Change Takes Time— So Start Today!

The last fifteen years have ushered in a period of change to rival even that of the industrial era in the nineteenth century. The Internet and other emerging technologies have forced a sea of change in every imaginable industry—banking, retail, hospitality, entertainment. Yet the housing industry remains stubbornly stuck in the past, clinging to outsized expectations born of 1950s post-war optimism and prosperity.

Ironically, many of the outside factors that led to that post-war era have converged once more today, though we find ourselves ill-prepared to take advantage. Our actions have, in fact, barred an entire generation of young adults from achieving the American Dream—a comfortable, financially-secure, middle-class life spent in a home of their own. Unlike their generational counterparts who came of age following the Great Depression and World War II, millennials will not be able to own a home—will barely be able to afford a roof over their heads at all—if we don't act now.

The consequences don't end there. Having fewer young buyers will cripple the already-stalled housing ladder, destroying the housing values—and by extension, the retirement—of baby boomers. The population rates, already in decline, will crater, leaving a dearth of able workers over the next several decades that will badly weaken America's economy.

If this sounds alarmist, it means we've already forgotten lessons taken from the Great Recession of 2008—overlooked, easily-dismissed problems can shake our nation to its very core. That crisis also centered on housing and, in fact, led to our current dilemma. Why? Because a "home of one's own" isn't just at the heart of the American Dream; it's the cornerstone of our way of life.

We need ten million new homes to solve the housing affordability problem. To do so, we'll need to re-insert the basic principles of supply and demand. This will require cooperation from every segment of our society—individuals, business leaders, communities, colleges and universities, the military, and every level of government. We need to consider solutions that are creative, perhaps even radical, and re-consider the very nature of what a home is and should be.

In this book I have presented eleven solutions as a starting point to conversations if this crisis is to be averted:

Radical Solution #1

Employer and corporation on-site housing villages.

This solution focuses on what used to be very common: living where you worked in an employer-provided, free or subsidized accommodation. (Learn more at CommercialHousingSolutions.com and on Twitter at #employerhousing).

Radical Solution #2

Retail conversion and retrofitting. This solution focuses on the existing infrastructure of deserted shopping malls and similar buildings that can be converted into mixed-use developments with a modern, walkable look, hidden garages, and retail fronts.

Radical Solution #3

Reshape our urban cores. This solution is possible by replacing parking spaces downtown with affordable housing. Let's put houses where cars used to be!

Radical Solution #4

Baby boomers, it's time to sell. This solution encourages the older generation to let go of their oversized houses and enjoy a downsized lifestyle—especially while property values are relatively high.

Radical Solution #5

ADUs, tiny homes, granny suites, and mobile communities. This minimalistic solution is for those who don't want to "keep up with the Joneses." It entails a proposal to relax Accessory Dwelling Units law to allow for rapid expansion of these alternative, functional types of homes and the lifestyles they enable.

Radical Solution #6

Endowment-sponsored housing. This solution will allow students and recent college graduates to live affordably *and* pay off their student debt faster.

Radical Solution #7

Freedom for developers. This solution suggest that we let developers work with urban planners to maximize the space available for housing. We must empower developers to return to affordable starter-home concepts.

Radical Solution #8

Tax incentives. This solution shows a plethora of possibilities to jumpstart affordable housing by changing property taxes.

Radical Solution #9

People first, then businesses. This solution represents a fresh approach to wooing large employers into our communities—by using state or local funds to build affordable housing communities for potential employees, instead of offering corporations bloated tax-incentive packages.

Radical Solution #10

Repurpose old military bases. This solution gives under-utilized military facilities new life by transforming them into starter-home developments.

Radical Solution #11

An innovative federal approach to financing home-ownership. This solution encompasses the revitalization and continuation of HUD programs, the widespread introduction of the 40-year mortgage, and willingness to leverage the weight of the executive branch to further the goal of ensuring a roof over every head.

The Ten-Year Plan

Simply discussing these options won't be enough. We need to act now to avoid missing out on the widespread growth and prosperity middle-class Americans experienced in the 1950s. As such, I have devised a ten-year plan as a model for how these solutions can be implemented.

2019

Employers: We must first involve the employers who are seeking employees in the midst of this season of all-time low unemployment rates. Increasing salary may help attract workers in this tough market, but it won't help ease the housing crunch that makes the cost-of-living so outrageous, particularly in tech havens like Silicon Valley. Instead, employers should consider creating everything from dormitory-style housing villages to single-family starter home neighborhoods as incentives to attract and retain employees.

Government at every level: Now is the time to introduce legislation and re-examine regulations and laws.

The federal level will need to create new laws that demand communities create non-government sponsored affordable housing. They should impose a minimum number of housing units in every community with twenty percent of them being designated as affordable housing. And finally, they will need to authorize the use of military land for low-cost housing.

The city and state levels will need to re-evaluate property tax codes to introduce new tax laws, as well as re-zone to allow granny apartments and temporary tiny houses on existing property. Lastly, they will need to start the conversation on better plans for the future, aligning visions and working on the flow of communication to ensure that the very best plans and solutions can be carried out.

2020

Colleges: Start developing plans to house a great number of former students by putting a plan in place for subsidized rents that will accelerate the reduction of student debt. Aim to have a certain percentage of recent graduates accepted into the program with the goal of home purchase—through money saved—in two years.

Baby boomers: Implement efforts to re-educate this demographic and help them find alternative housing that they can afford. With boomers retiring at the pace of ten thousand *per day,* this step cannot be ignored for long.

2021

Federal government: This is the critical year—BRAC will release its recommendations for new base closures. We have eight hundred bases covering millions and millions of acres. We need to seriously consider those locations the Pentagon wants to close, *and* we need to convert those locations to affordable housing.

2022–2024

Here comes a crucial juncture. We don't know what interest rates are going to be, but we know many people will start taking Social Security while fewer will be paying in, due to population effects.

As a nation, we will likely be facing an economic slowdown. But real estate has always been an important part of the GDP. We need plans in place to build millions of starter homes locally and quickly, because at this point, the greatest demographic in the country will be men and women turning 65. Baby boomers will be retiring, cashing out their too-large homes, and moving into smaller, maintenance-free homes—if we built them. We need to encourage this shift, but we also need to prepare for it. Urban conversions will begin to take shape as autonomous vehicles and alternative transportation methods take hold. Cities will play a critical role in bringing affordable living space where cars used to be parked.

2025–2027

If the plans listed so far have worked, we'll start to see the fruits of the labor here. Housing may still be in crisis, but it will be much less of a crisis than it was in the past. At this point, we can start thinking more about urban planning and how to map out our cities in ways that will continue to encourage proper development.

2027–2029

If we've chosen not to act or if we've waited for someone else to solve the problem, here is the stage where we'll look back and realize we're in an even greater crisis. Affordability will have decreased as the supply and demand chain becomes impossibly unbalanced. Only drastic action from the government will be able to solve it, though the damage will already be done. We'll have lost a decade that could have resulted in 1950s-style growth and prosperity that could have reset the shrinking middle class.

The Future Is Still Bright

Despite my grim predictions, I remain optimistic that we can solve this crisis. But I have been in real estate—and on this earth—long enough to know that many people will resist these ideas, and indeed, any changes. Some will do so purely out of self-interest. Even a broken system benefits someone, and those who profit have no interest in working against their own profit. Others will dismiss our housing shortage as someone else's problem, one to be solved after they're gone.

For millennials, however, the problem is immediate. We are facing a critical shortage of homes for first-time buyers, and this will soon impact every aspect of American life. Increasingly, millennials and their political allies are realizing this—hence, the birth and rise of the YIMBY (Yes In My Back Yard) movement to counter the NIMBY (Not In My Back Yard) movement of yesteryear.[96]

Indeed, as with so many societal challenges we currently face, the onus will be on this young generation to solve it. Luckily, they may be the *ideal* generation to solve it.

Among the many generalizations made about millennials is that they have little interest in status quo and tradition. What some consider a symptom of entitlement, others have called an admirable freedom of thought and spirit. More than one media outlet has referred to millennials as the "Ben Franklin generation."[97] The solutions presented in this book require out-of-the-box thinking that challenges years of practice and the mentality that "this is the way we do things around here"—and the millennials as a whole seem especially well-suited to accept that challenge.

Taken collectively, millennials have shown themselves as willing to re-evaluate and even subvert established norms when it comes to relationships, the nine-to-five work schedule, transportation, and entertainment. Never are those qualities more needed than now. They face a daunting challenge, certainly, but also a unique opportunity. Millennials can make fundamental, lasting change to a broken system and leave the country in better shape for their futures, and for the futures of generations that come after them.

WORKBOOK

Conclusion Questions

Question: In your own words, how would you describe the current and looming housing crisis to someone who doesn't believe that there is a problem? How can the public be educated so as to affect change without creating panic?

_____

_____

_____

_____

_____

_____

_____

_____

_____

Question: Which of the author's eleven radical solutions are you the most able to address through your own housing choices and within your spheres of influence? How will you take steps to be a champion for this idea?

_____

_____

_____

_____

_____

_____

_____

_____

_____

_____

_____

Question: Solving our nation's looming housing crisis will take cooperation between political parties, business entities, older and younger generations, and the various special interest groups that make up our society. How does solving this housing problem benefit everyone? What steps can be taken to help groups that are normally antagonistic toward each other choose to work together for the common good?

_____

_____

_____

_____

_____

_____

_____

_____

_____

_____

_____

Action: Review the eleven radical solutions as well as the timeline. Then create your own timeline for how you plan to work for change within your community and sphere of influence.

REFERENCES

Notes

1. "Radical." *Oxford Living Dictionaries.* https://en.oxforddictionaries.com/definition/radical.

2. "Housing." *Merriam-Webster.* https://www.merriam-webster.com/dictionary/housing.

3. Whitman, Walt. "New York Dissected." *Life Illustrated.* July 19, 1856, p. 93. In *The Walt Whitman Archive.* https://whitmanarchive.org/published/periodical/journalism/tei/per.00270.html.

4. Connley, Courtney. "A New Study Says an Overwhelming Majority of Millennials Want to Be Homeowners, but Student Loans Are Holding Them Back." *CNBC.com.* December 8, 2018. https://www.cnbc.com/2018/12/08/student-loan-burden-barring-millenials-from-home-ownership-study.html?__source=iosappshare%7Ccom.google.Gmail.ShareExtension.

5. Ingram, Christopher. "The One Surefire Way to Grow Your Wealth in the U.S." *Washington Post Wonkblog.* September 28, 2017. https://www.washingtonpost.com/news/wonk/wp/2017/09/28/the-one-surefire-way-to-grow-your-wealth-in-the-u-s/?noredirect=on&utm_term=.803ffccc8875.

6. Derived from "Home Ownership Is the Engine of American Wealth," graph. In Ingraham, "The One Surefire Way to Grow Your Wealth in the U.S.," *Washington Post Wonkblog*. Info from Federal Reserve Board.

7. Amadeo, Kimberly. "Stock Market Crash of 1929 Facts, Causes, and Impact: The Worst Crash in U.S. History." *The Balance*. October 12, 2018. https://www.thebalance.com/stock-market-crash-of-1929-causes-effects-and-facts-3305891.

8. Suddath, Claire. "The Crash of 1929." *Time*. October 29, 2008. http://content.time.com/time/nation/article/0,8599,1854569,00.html.

9. Frankel, Matthew. "9 Baby-Boomer Statistics That Will Blow You Away." *The Motley Fool*. July 29, 2017. https://www.fool.com/retirement/2017/07/29/9-baby-boomer-statistics-that-will-blow-you-away.aspx.

10. "Median Household Incomes." *Stanford University*. https://web.stanford.edu/class/polisci120a/immigration/Median%20Household%20Income.pdf.

11. "57% of Americans Have Less Than $1,000 in Savings." *PR Newswire.com. GO Banking Rates*. September 12, 2017. https://www.prnewswire.com/news-releases/57-of-americans-have-less-than-1000-in-savings-300516664.html.

12. "Millennials." *Pew Research Center*. http://www.pewresearch.org/topics/millennials.

13. "American Generation Fast Facts." *CNN.com*. September 4, 2018. https://www.cnn.com/2013/11/06/us/baby-boomer-generation-fast-facts/index.html.

14. Derived from "Share of Owner-Occupied Housing: Year Structure Built," graph. In Na Zhao, "The Aging Housing Stock," *Eye on Housing*, National Association of Home Builders (August 11, 2015). Info from U.S. Census Bureau, *American Housing Survey*, Department of Housing and

Urban Development, 2013. https://eyeonhousing.org/2015/08/the-aging-housing-stock-2.

15. "Measures of Central Tendency for Wage Data." *SocialSecurity.gov.* https://www.ssa.gov/oact/cola/central.html.

16. "Quarterly Residential Vacancies and Homeownership, Second Quarter, 2018." *US Census Bureau.* July 26, 2018. https://www.census.gov/housing/hvs/files/currenthvspress.pdf.

17. Nova, Annie. "These Are the Reasons Why Millions of Millennials Can't Buy Houses." *CNBC.com.* July 11, 2018. https://www.cnbc.com/2018/07/09/these-are-the-reasons-why-millions-of-millennials-cant-buy-houses.html.

18. Derived from "Annual Births in the United States (1945–2010)," graph, Joint Center for Housing Studies of Harvard University, *Housing Perspectives.* In Michael T. Robinson, "The Generations," *CareerPlanner.com.* Info from United States Census Bureau and the National Vital Statistics Report. https://www.careerplanner.com/Career-Articles/Generations.cfm.

19. Hamilton, Brady E., Joyce A. Martin, Michelle J. K. Osterman, Anne K. Driscoll, and Lauren M. Rossen. "Births: Provisional Data for 2017." *Centers for Disease Control.* May 2018. https://www.cdc.gov/nchs/data/vsrr/report004.pdf.

20. Hamilton, Martin, Osterman, Driscoll, and Rossen, "Births: Provision Data for 2017."

21. Roser, Max. "Fertility Rate." *Our World in Data.* 2014. Revised December 2, 2017. https://ourworldindata.org/fertility-rate.

22. Bluejay, Michael. "Long-Term Real Estate Appreciation in the US." *MichaelBlujay.com.* August 2009. https://michaelbluejay.com/house/appreciation.html.

23. Kusisto, Laura. "The Next Housing Crisis: A Historic Shortage of New Homes." *The Wall Street Journal.* March

18, 2018. https://www.wsj.com/articles/american-housing-shortage-slams-the-door-on-buyers-1521395460.

24. "United States Housing Starts." Graph. *TradingEconomics.com.* March 8, 2019. https://tradingeconomics.com/united-states/housing-starts.

25. Derived from "Median Age of Owner-Occupied Housing," graph. In Josh Miller, "The Aging Housing Stock," *Eye on Housing*, National Association of Home Builders (January 20, 2014). Info from U.S. Census Bureau, *American Housing Survey*, Department of Housing and Urban Development, 2011.

26. Kusisto, "The Next Housing Crisis."

27. Thompson, Derek. "The Go-Nowhere Generation Speaks: 'I'd Love to Move, but I Can't'." *TheAtlantic.com.* March 15, 2012. https://www.theatlantic.com/business/archive/2012/03/the-go-nowhere-generation-speaks-id-love-to-move-but-i-cant/254579/.

28. Gaffney, Jacob. "Millennials Will Purchase at Least 10 Million New Homes in the Next 10 Years." *HousingWire.com.* https://www.housingwire.com/articles/47667-millennials-will-purchase-at-least-10-million-new-homes-in-the-next-10-years.

29. "United States Housing Starts," graph, *TradingEconomics.com.*

30. Collins, Jeff. "Southern California Needs Nearly 1 Million Affordable Homes, Report Says." *Orange County Register.* May 16, 2018. https://www.ocregister.com/2018/05/16/southern-california-needs-nearly-1-million-affordable-homes-report-says.

31. Snyderman, Robin. "Making the Case for Employer-Assisted Housing." *Shelterforce.* May 1, 2005. https://shelterforce.org/2005/05/01/making-the-case-for-employer-assisted-housing.

32. Kendall, Marisa. "Work in Tech? Want to Own a Home? Here's an Idea." *Mercury News.* March 30, 2018. https://www.mercurynews.com/2018/03/30/work-in-tech-want-to-own-a-home-move-to-pittsburgh-bay-area-billboard-says.

33. "Work Opportunity Tax Credit." United States Department of Labor. https://www.doleta.gov/business/incentives/opptax.

34. Weber, Christopher. "America's Homeless Population Rises for the First Time in Years." *AP News.* December 6, 2017. https://www.apnews.com/47662ad74baf4bb09f40619e4fd25a94.

35. Smith, Liz. "What Is the Average Savings Account Balance." *SmartAsset.com.* August 20, 2018. https://smartasset.com/checking-account/savings-account-average-balance.

36. Sherman, Erik. "5 Hard Facts about Walmart's Touted New $11 Entry Wage." *Forbes.com.* January 14, 2018. https://www.forbes.com/sites/eriksherman/2018/01/14/4-hard-facts-about-walmarts-touted-new-11-entry-wage/#11f4f7bc6660s.

37. "Lincoln, NE Rental Market Trends." *RentCafe.* October 2018. https://www.rentcafe.com/average-rent-market-trends/us/ne/lincoln.

38. Thomas, Lauren. "The Amount of Retail Space Closing in 2018 Is on Pace to Break a Record." *CNBC.* April 18, 2018. https://www.cnbc.com/2018/04/18/the-amount-of-retail-space-closing-in-2018-is-on-pace-to-break-record.html.

39. Grasso, David. "Repurposed Retail Space Is the Affordable Housing of the Future." *Bold.* February 17, 2016. https://bold.global/david-grasso/2016/02/17/repurposed-retail-space-is-the-affordable-housing-of-the-future.

40. McCoy, Terrence. "The Future of Suburban Homelessness? As Malls Empty, an Old Macy's Becomes

a Homeless Shelter." *Washington Post.* July 6, 2018. https://www.washingtonpost.com/news/inspired-life/wp/2018/07/06/americas-malls-are-emptying-so-this-vacant-macys-became-a-homeless-shelter/?noredirect=on&utm_term=.cfb43d9fd835.

41. Kimmelman, Michael. "Paved, but Still Alive." *New York Times.* January 6, 2012. https://www.nytimes.com/2012/01/08/arts/design/taking-parking-lots-seriously-as-public-spaces.html.

42. Lindeman, Tracey. "In Some US Cities, There Are Over Ten Times More Parking Spaces Than Households." *Motherboard.* July 18, 2018. https://motherboard.vice.com/en_us/article/d3epmm/parking-spots-outnumber-homes-us-cities.

43. Plumer, Brad. "Cars Take Up Way Too Much Space in Cities. New Technology Could Change That." *Vox.* https://www.vox.com/a/new-economy-future/cars-cities-technologies.

44. Kimmelman, "Paved but Still Alive."

45. "Housing Trends Since 1950." *David Ramsey.* https://www.daveramsey.com/blog/housing-trends.

46. Cited in Deborah Kearns. "Baby Boomers Are Struggling to Downsize—and It Could Create the Next Housing Crisis," *CNBC* (September 11, 2018). https://www.cnbc.com/2018/09/11/baby-boomers-are-struggling-to-downsize--and-it-could-create-the-next-housing-crisis.html.

47. Hurd, Michael D. and Susann Rohwedder. "Effects of the Financial Crisis and Great Recession on American Households." *National Bureau of Economic Research.* September 2010. https://www.nber.org/papers/w16407.

48. Bloom, Esther. "Here's How Much Money the Average Homebuyer Makes." *CNBC.* April 25, 2017. https://www.cnbc.com/2017/04/25/heres-how-much-money-the-average-first-time-home-buyer-makes.html.

49. Erb, Kelly Phillips. "9 Tax-Related Myths About Selling Your Home." *Forbes.com.* October 10, 2012. https://www.forbes.com/sites/kellyphillipserb/2012/10/10/9-tax-related-myths-about-selling-your-home/#57c38c5378b4.

50. Social Security Administration. "Monthly Statistical Snapshot, September 2018." October 2018. https://www.ssa.gov/policy/docs/quickfacts/stat_snapshot.

51. "What Is the Tiny House Movement?" *The Tiny Life.* https://thetinylife.com/what-is-the-tiny-house-movement.

52. Chen, James. "Accessory Dwelling Unit (ADU)." *Investopedia.com.* July 30, 2018. https://www.investopedia.com/terms/a/accessory-dwelling-unit-adu.asp#ixzz5Fam6Nslz.

53. Cohen, Josh. "California ADU Applications Skyrocket After Regulatory Reform." *NextCity.org.* January 4, 2018. https://nextcity.org/daily/entry/california-adu-applications-skyrocket-after-regulatory-reform.

54. Flint, Anthony. "How One Colorado City Instantly Created Affordable Housing." *Citylab.com.* May 17, 2016. https://www.citylab.com/design/2016/05/how-one-colorado-city-instantly-created-affordable-housing/483027/.

55. AARP's 58-page report on ADUs, "Accessory Dwelling Units: State Act and Local Ordinance," written by the American Planning Association and first published in 2000, contains invaluable information about the creation of a viable ADU program. https://www.aarp.org/content/dam/aarp/livable-communities/documents-2015/ADU-report-AARP-APA.pdf.

56. Based on cover image from Rodney L. Cobb and Scott Dvorak, *Accessory Dwelling Units: Model State Act and Local Ordinance*, Public Policy Institute, AARP, 2000. https://assets.aarp.org/rgcenter/consume/d17158_dwell.pdf.

57. May, Leonard. "ADU and OAU Priorities and Whom Policies Benefit. *Boulder Weekly*. March 15, 2018. https://www.boulderweekly.com/opinion/adu-oau-priorities-policies-benefit.

58. Garrick, David. "Judge Orders San Diego to Stop Ticketing Homeless Living in Vehicles." *The San Diego Union-Tribune*. August 22, 2018. https://www.sandiegouniontribune.com/news/politics/sd-me-homeless-vehicle-20180822-story.html.

59. Pollard, Amy. "Living Behind the Wheel." *Slate.com*. August 20, 2018. https://slate.com/business/2018/08/vehicular-homelessness-is-on-the-rise-should-cities-help-people-sleep-in-their-cars.html.

60. Reggev, Kate. "10 Modern Prefab Homes That Cost Less Than $100,000." *Dwell.com*. June 26, 2018. https://www.dwell.com/article/affordable-prefab-homes-a16a5c98.

61. Derek Earl. "42 Ways You Can Make Money and Travel the World." *Wanderingearl.com*. February 18, 2013. https://www.wanderingearl.com/42-ways-you-can-make-money-and-travel-the-world/.

62. Rechtshaffen, Ted. "Renting During Retirement? 10 Cases Where It Might Be Right for You." *Financial Post*. January 27, 2015. https://business.financialpost.com/personal-finance/renting-during-retirement-10-cases-where-it-might-be-right-for-you.

63. Dickler, Jessica. "Student Loan Balances Jump Nearly 150 Percent in a Decade." *CNBC*. August 29, 2017. https://www.cnbc.com/2017/08/29/student-loan-balances-jump-nearly-150-percent-in-a-decade.html.

64. Tuttle, Brad. "New College Graduates May Be Looking at the Highest Starting Salaries Ever." *TIME*. May 12, 2017. http://time.com/money/4777074/college-grad-pay-2017-average-salary.

65. Friedman, Zack. "Student Loan Debt Statistics In 2018: A

$1.5 Trillion Crisis." *Forbes.* June 13, 2018. https://www.forbes.com/sites/zackfriedman/2018/06/13/st udent-loan-debt-statistics-2018/#3b0184f27310.

66. Berman, Jillian, and Jay Zehngebot. "Paying for Your College, 30 Years Ago vs. Today." *Market Watch.* November 21, 2017. https://www.marketwatch.com/ graphics/college-debt-now-and-then.

67. Friedman, Zack. "Student Loan Debt Statistics in 2018: A $1.5 Trillion Crisis." *Forbes.* June 13, 2018. https://www.forbes.com/sites/zackfriedman/2018/06/13/st udent-loan-debt-statistics-2018/#3b0184f27310.

68. Lorin, Janet. "University Endowments." *Bloomberg.* December 26, 2017. https://www.bloomberg.com/ quicktake/university-endowments.

69. Powell, Farran. "10 Universities with the Biggest Endowments." *US News and World Report.* October 16, 2018. https://www.usnews.com/education/best-colleges/the-short-list-college/articles/10-universities-with-the-biggest-endowments.

70. Lobosco, Katie. "Why Colleges with Large Endowments Still Charge Tuition." *CNN.* November 4, 2016. https://money.cnn.com/2016/11/04/pf/college/endowment s-financial-aid/index.html.

71. Cited in Connley, "A New Study Says an Overwhelming Majority of Millennials Want to Be Homeowners."

72. Hess, Abigail. "Here's How Much the Average Student Loan Borrower Owes When They Graduate." *CNBC.* February 15, 2018. https://www.cnbc.com/2018/02/15/heres-how-much-the-average-student-loan-borrower-owes-when-they-graduate.html.

73. Kusisto, "The Next Housing Crisis."

74. Kusisto, "The Next Housing Crisis."

75. Kimberlin, Sara, Laura Tach, and Christopher Wimer. "A

Renter's Tax Credit to Curtail the Affordable Housing Crisis." *RSF: The Russell Sage Foundation Journal of the Social Sciences*, 4, no. 2 (2018), p. 131–160.

76. Stevens, Laura, Keiko Morris, and Katie Honan. "Amazon Picks New York City, Northern Virginia for Its HQ2 Locations." *Wall Street Journal.* November 13, 2018. https://www.wsj.com/articles/amazon-chooses-new-york-city-and-northern-virginia-for-additional-headquarters-1542075336.

77. Soper, Spencer. "Amazon Scraps Plan to Build a Headquarters in New York City." *Bloomberg.* February 14, 2019. https://www.bloomberg.com/news/articles/2019-02-14/amazon-says-it-won-t-build-a-headquarters-in-new-york-city.

78. Eaglen, Mackenzie. "Closing Old Military Bases Will Help Our Defense—and Our Communities." *The Hill.* July 28, 2017. https://thehill.com/blogs/pundits-blog/the-military/344321-closing-old-military-bases-will-help-our-defense-and-our.

79. "The Philadelphia Navy Yard as a Model of Resilience and Re-invention." Supplement to presentation by Alan Greenberger. *World Heritage City Initiative.* https://globalphiladelphia.org/sites/globalphiladelphia.org/files/NavyYardExecutiveSummary.pdf.

80. Kiersz, Andy. "Here's How Much Land Military Bases Take Up in Each State." *Business Insider.* November 10, 2014. https://www.businessinsider.com/how-much-land-military-bases-take-up-in-each-state-2014-11.

81. Clarke, Sara K. "A Tale of Two Neighborhoods." *Orlando Sentinel.* March 4, 2008. https://www.orlandosentinel.com/news/os-xpm-2008-03-04-annex04-story.html.

82. sadf Adapted from Kiersz, "Here's How Much Land Military Bases Take Up in Each State," chart, info from Department of Defense.

83. Olmstead, Molly. "Report: Ben Carson's New HUD Mission Statement to Emphasize Self-Sufficiency, Ignore Discrimination." *Slate.* March 7, 2018. https://slate.com/news-and-politics/2018/03/ben-carson-reportedly-to-release-new-hud-mission-statement-that-focuses-on-self-sufficiency.html.

84. "Mission." *HUD.gov.* https://www.hud.gov/about/mission.

85. Kingsley, Thomas G. "Trends in Housing Problems and Federal Housing Assistance." *Urban Institute.* October 2017. https://www.urban.org/sites/default/files/publication/94146/trends-in-housing-problems-and-federal-housing-assistance.pdf.

86. Lockert, Melanie. "How Student Loans Impact Your Debt-to-Income Ratio." *Student Loan Hero.* March 14, 2016. https://studentloanhero.com/featured/student-loan-debt-to-income-ratio/.

87. Passy, Jacob. "What the Fed's Rate Hike Will Mean for America's Wavering Housing Market." *Market Watch.* December 21, 2018. https://www.marketwatch.com/story/why-2019-wont-lead-to-a-home-buyers-market-2018-11-28.

88. Pritchard, Justin. "Pros and Cons of a 40 Year Mortgage." *The Balance.* November 2, 2018. https://www.thebalance.com/40-year-mortgages-315652.

89. "Executive Orders." *Federal Register.* August 15, 2016. https://www.archives.gov/federal-register/codification/executive-order/11063.html.

90. Zilbert, Mark. "The Blockchain for Real Estate, Explained." *Forbes.com.* April 28, 2018. https://www.forbes.com/sites/forbesrealestatecouncil/2018/04/23/the-blockchain-for-real-estate-explained/#10af274781eb.

91. Stewart, Jack. "Uber Unveils the Flying Taxi It Wants to Rule the Skies." *Wired.* May 8, 2018.

https://www.wired.com/story/uber-unveils-flying-taxi.

92. Plyer, Allison. "Facts for Features: Katrina Impact." *The Data Center.* August 26, 2016. https://www.datacenterresearch.org/data-resources/katrina/facts-for-impact/.

93. Hunn, David, Matt Dempsey, and Mihir Zaveri. "Harvey's Floods." *Houston Chronicle.* March 30, 2018. https://www.houstonchronicle.com/news/article/In-Harvey-s-deluge-most-damaged-homes-were-12794820.php.

94. Hill, Catey. "43% of U.S. Homes Are at High Risk of Natural Disaster." *Market Watch.* September 3, 2015. https://www.marketwatch.com/story/43-of-us-homes-are-at-high-risk-of-natural-disaster-2015-09-03.

95. "Coastal States at Risk from Global Sea Level Rise." Graph. In *Union of Concerned Scientists.* Info from Strauss et al., National Oceanic and Atomospheric Administration, 2012A (2012). https://www.ucsusa.org/sites/default/files/images/2015/08/gw-impacts-graphic-coastal-states-at-risk-from-global-sea-level-rise.jpg.

96. McCormick, Erin. "Rise of the Yimbys: The Angry Millennials with a Radical Housing Solution." *The Guardian.* October 2, 2017. https://www.theguardian.com/cities/2017/oct/02/rise-of-the-yimbys-angry-millennials-radical-housing-solution.

97. Hanft, Adam. "The Stunning Evolution of Millennials: They've Become the Ben Franklin Generation." *Huffington Post.* November 7, 2014. https://www.huffingtonpost.com/adam-hanft/the-stunning-evolution-of_b_6108412.html.

A Note from the Author

Thank you for picking up a copy of this book.

There are two key moments that brought me to this place of writing a book about housing. First is an interesting story about me attending the national housing meeting in downtown San Diego in 2017.

On purpose, I stayed about a mile away from the convention, because I like to walk in cities, and San Diego is a beautiful city. The meeting I was attending was a gathering of some of the smartest people in our country regarding housing. The shocking truth was, each morning I walked to the conference, I passed a large number of homeless people in downtown San Diego. It was a stroke of irony to pass so many homeless people while walking to a gathering of the nation's smartest people about housing.

If that doesn't shock you into writing something, I don't know what does. It made me recall the times in my life when I've been close to homeless, nearly broke, or the many times I've moved, or slept on somebody's couch before I got on my feet.

The second reason for writing this book was that it was time to reflect back on my successful career. I wanted to put forth my real-life experiences in book format to provide very real solutions for American real estate, intertwined with stories and facts about life and my career.

My ultimate goal in writing *Radical Housing Solutions* is to increase the number of homeowners, more specifically among our younger generations. It is also my sincere hope that you learn something that can help you bring about change in your community. Everyone should have the freedom and opportunity to live out their American dream, and owning a home is the backbone of making this dream a reality. For some, it's a way to build wealth. For others, stability.

While it may not be obvious at first sight how some of these radical solutions will help you buy a home, each idea is envisioned as a stepping stone to kickstart the housing market. Any increase in the number of places someone can live affordably will improve your chances of purchasing a home. Perhaps you personally will benefit by paying down your student loan or saving for that down payment when one of these solutions is implemented in your city.

Maybe your heart is to help our most vulnerable. In many ways, our homeless crisis in America is one of the most pressing issues of our time. More housing for all incomes can only help improve putting a roof over every person's head, whether they can afford it or not. Together, we can certainly try.

If you know me, you know I'm a man of action. So, it's not enough just to put these solutions on paper. I want to see this through, and I'm passionate to give back. I hope this passion will come through on these pages for you as my reader. Let's do what we can to help our friends, our neighbors, and our family members.

We simply must solve our affordability crisis and bring shelter to all who need it. I believe that, if many of these Radical Housing Solutions are adopted, we can come out of the other end of the housing crisis to save this next generation of young families. We're all in this together.

You can learn more about my biography on our websites:

- RadicalHousing.com
- CommercialHousingSolutions.com

Acknowledgments

A lifetime of gaining experience and perspective only comes when you allow others to help you. Sometimes, you don't know until many years later that somebody has had an influence on you. In many cases, it's obvious when someone reaches out to help—but you have to be smart enough to pay attention. So, as I go down the list of people I want to thank for shaping me, I'll invariably forget many people I should acknowledge. Please forgive me if that is you.

First, I want to thank my mom, Nancy, who for many years taught me about the power of making the most out of what little you may have in your possession. She also taught me the value of risk and reward, as well as the reality that you must keep moving forward with a positive mindset, regardless of the circumstances. My first experiences of real estate were with her in the late seventies, when she proudly got her GED, became a real estate agent, and taught me the hard lessons of the residential rental business.

I also must acknowledge and thank my dad, who is no longer with us, for his love for me later in life when we were both old enough to enjoy being friends.

To my brother Mike and my sister Marie: please forgive me for all of the bad business deals I talked you into as kids, so I could rid you of your hard-earned allowance. Also, thanks for letting me beat you in Monopoly over and over again. Being the older brother has its advantages.

While I'm on the subject of family, I want to acknowledge my second-generation Italian heritage and give thanks to the families who made the long, hard trip to this new world: the Bonitatis, Rampinos, Marinis, and Monacos.

Thanks also to my Aunt Maggie and Uncle Hal, who let me live with them after high school when I left home and headed west. It was their generosity that I've been able to pay forward even to this day, housing and hosting so many friends and family members over the years.

My conversation about family would not be complete without including my spiritual family and friends. God's continual blessings, forgiveness, and gift of eternal life have been a huge part of my core beliefs and have shaped me to be who I am today.

So many people have influenced me from my early education through the nearly forty years of my working life. I've held many different kinds of jobs over the years, from sweeping floors to cooking burgers to loading building supplies. But my favorites were the many sales jobs I've had. You name it, I've sold it: lollipops, balloons, ice cream, pots and pans, magazines, lawn mowers, washing machines, insurance, and millions upon millions of dollars of real estate.

In each of those experiences, there has been someone important who trained me, helped me—or even fired me!

From my earlier work life, I want to thank Bob Carr, Ed Chaffin, Robert Bell, Bill Canfield, and Teddy the rock guy. The lessons I learned from Teddy when I was 16 could fill a book of their own.

In my current role, I've been helped by many people as well, but three stand out as the most influential: John Gray, Kay Hill, and Jon Good.

I'm also grateful for the many people who encouraged and helped me take on the project of a book—specifically, Janet Edmunson, John Hawkins, and Mike Travis, along with his brother George.

Being a dad is certainly one of the highlights of life, but who knew your kids teach you as much as you teach them? For my son Joey and me, that moment came when he taught me a valuable lesson in the middle of the Badlands, South Dakota—this story could fill yet another book. My daughter Alicia, who is the most precious thing on this planet, has blessed me with her timely and wonderful insights. Thank you both so much!

Finally, I must thank my lovely wife of thirty years, Carolyn. Without her years of encouragement, boldness, teaching, and forgiveness, I would most certainly not be where I am now. Thank you again for getting me through college algebra and for putting up with me whenever it was time to sell another one of our many homes.

Thank you all—and again, all those I didn't name as well. Your influence has meant so much.

About the Author

I'm Tony Bonitati, the founder of Commercial Housing Solutions. I envisioned Commercial Housing Solutions after recognizing that the unavailability of affordable housing was negatively impacting both employers and the current workforce.

I am a broker and shareholder with NAI Earle Furman, and I founded the firm's Multifamily Division, which specializes in cultivating investor relationships throughout the country to leverage multi-million-dollar transactions.

My sales background includes services in The Work

Number verification, I-9, unemployment tax services, and HR-and payroll-related solutions. I bring well over three decades of business experience to identifying and implementing win-win solutions.

My Story

To help you understand my heart in writing this book, I'll share some details about my personal story.

Let's start by saying my background is a little out of the ordinary. I'm left-handed, so that tells you right off the bat that I do most things backwards. Work has been a part of me from a young age: cutting grass, shoveling snow, you name it. By the time I was 12, I was already practically an expert at yard work. Fast forward to my many jobs, working my way through college, graduating from Arizona State with a degree in finance.

I grew up idolizing Michael J. Fox's character on the TV show *Family Ties*, Alex P. Keaton, who strutted around confidently with a shirt and tie on while the rest of his family espoused larger theory about society.

However, I also grew up with a bronze picture of John F. Kennedy on the wall. Kennedy was idolized by so many when I very young. He was assassinated the year before I was born, so I was a mixed bag politically growing up. Then, in 1984, I had the privilege of voting in the presidential election for the first time, and, of course, I voted for Ronald Reagan—who didn't? After all, 1984 was a wonderful year to be an American. We had come out of a bad recession, and things were looking bright. Of course, it helped that I was 20 years old in 1984 and free to live where ever I wanted!

My political life stayed mostly a mixed bag after that, up until recent memory. Over the course of the last three presidential elections, I've voted for both major parties and a third-party candidate. I voted for President Barack Obama, but I also voted for President Donald Trump. I believe Barack Obama is a man of high caliber, and it was a privilege to vote for him and have his family in the white house.

My main reason for voting for President Trump was because he was an outsider. We needed someone different to shake things up—boy, who knew it was going to be this crazy? Having grown up near New York in the Eighties, I have always been very aware that Trump is a brash real estate tycoon. So, as a real estate guy myself, I thought housing was becoming a major issue in our country, and I hoped Trump would mandate the end of the red tape and help us all live more affordably.

I envisioned *Radical Housing Solutions* after recognizing that the unavailability of affordable housing was negatively impacting both employers and the current workforce.

My vast experience in commercial real estate, development, and housing offers a unique perspective to companies evaluating the cost-benefit analysis of providing employer-subsidized housing to their employees. I have created a replicable, yet incredibly client-specific model for remedying the divide between income and affordable housing.

Professional Achievements and Accolades

- 2018 Capital Club
- 2017 #1 Broker in Sales (Co-Lead) for NAI Earle Furman
- 2017 Largest Transaction Award
- 2017 & 2016 Capital Club, Diamond Award (highest-tier sales award)
- 2016 & 2014 CoStar Power Broker Award
- 2015 & 2013 Capital Club, Platinum Award
- 2012 Largest Transaction Award
- 2012 Capital Club
- TALX/Equifax Workforce Solutions
- 2007 & 2004 Service Excellence Award (over 100% of quota)
- 2005 Grand Slam Award
- 2005 Highest Percentage Quota (The Work Number)
- 2003 100% Quota (Fiscal Year) Award

How to Contact Tony

Twitter & Instagram

@tonybonitati (#radicalhousing)

Facebook

https://m.facebook.com/Tony-Bonitati-337929590382457/?ref=bookmarks

Radicalhousing.com

Commericalhousingsolutions.com

About Speak It To Book

Speak It to Book, the premier ghostwriting agency and publisher for faith-filled thought leaders, is revolutionizing how books are created and used.

We are a team of world-changing people who are passionate about making your great ideas famous.

Imagine:

- What if you had a way to beat writer's block, overcome your busy schedule, and get all of those ideas out of your head?

- What if you could partner with a team to crush lack of motivation and productivity so you can get your story in front of the people who need it most?

- What if you took that next step into significance and influence, using your book to launch your platform?

- What if you could write your book with a team of professionals from start to finish?

Your ideas are meant for a wider audience. Visit www.speakittobook.com to schedule a call with our team of Jesus-loving publishing professionals today.

Made in the USA
Columbia, SC
03 April 2019